BEST
EDITORIAL

OF THE YEAR

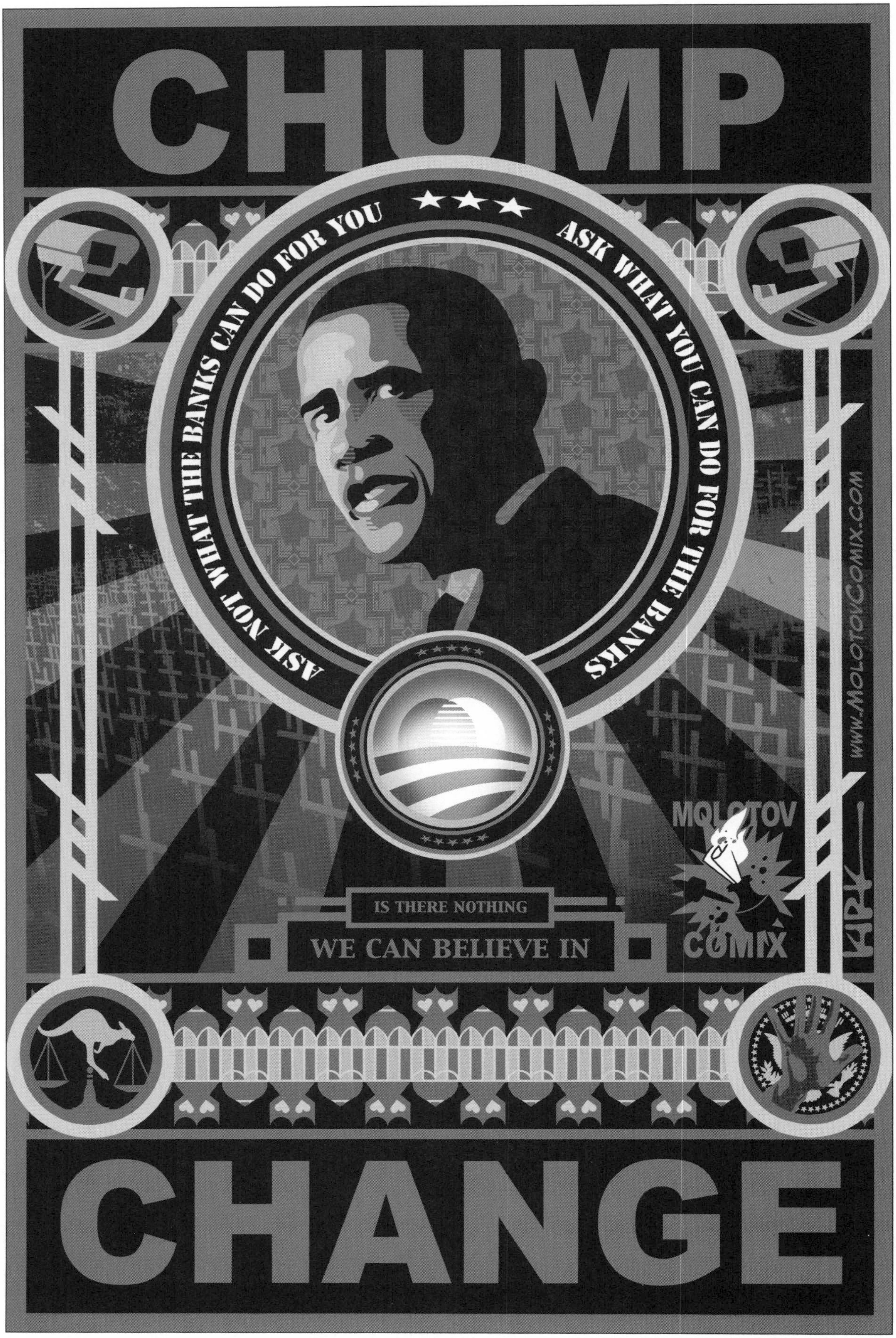
CHUMP
ASK NOT WHAT THE BANKS CAN DO FOR YOU
ASK WHAT YOU CAN DO FOR THE BANKS
IS THERE NOTHING
WE CAN BELIEVE IN
MOLOTOV
COMIX
WWW.MOLOTOVCOMIX.COM
KIRK
CHANGE

KIRK ANDERSON
Courtesy KIRKtoons.com

BEST EDITORIAL CARTOONS OF THE YEAR

2011 EDITION

Edited by
CHARLES BROOKS

PELICAN PUBLISHING COMPANY
Gretna 2011

Library of Congress Serial Catalog Data

Best Editorial Cartoons, 1972-
Gretna [La.] Pelican Pub. Co.
v. 39 cm annual—
"A pictorial history of the year."

United States—Politics and Government—
1969—Caricatures and Cartoons—Periodicals.
E839.5.B45 320.9'7309240207 73-643645
ISSN 0091-2220   MARC-S

Printed in the United States of America
Published by Pelican Publishing Company, Inc.
1000 Burmaster Street, Gretna, Louisiana 70053

Contents

Award-Winning Cartoons

2010 PULITZER PRIZE

MARK FIORE

Animated Political Cartoonist
SFGate.com

Began his career drawing traditional newspaper editorial cartoons; in the late 1990s started experimenting with animating political cartoons; following a brief period as editorial cartoonist at the *San Jose Mercury-News,* decided to concentrate on animation; now called by *The Wall Street Journal* "the undisputed guru of the form"; his animated political cartoons are featured on the *San Francisco Chronicle's* web site, SFGate.com; winner of the 2004 Robert F. Kennedy Journalism Award and twice honored by the National Cartoonists Society for his work in new media.

MIKE PETERS

Editorial Cartoonist
Dayton Daily News

Staff artist for the *Chicago Daily News* in his early career; mentored by renowned World War II cartoonist Bill Mauldin; named editorial cartoonist for the *Dayton Daily News* in 1969; in collaboration with his wife, Marian, in 1984 created the award-winning "Mother Goose & Grimm" comic strip, which appears in more than 800 newspapers worldwide; recipient of numerous awards, including the Sigma Delta Chi Award in 1975, the Pulitzer Prize in 1981, and previous Headliner Awards in 1983, 1988, and 1993; awarded the honorary Doctor of Humane Letters degree in 1998 by the University of Dayton; syndicated by King Features.

2009 SIGMA DELTA CHI AWARD
(Awarded in 2010)

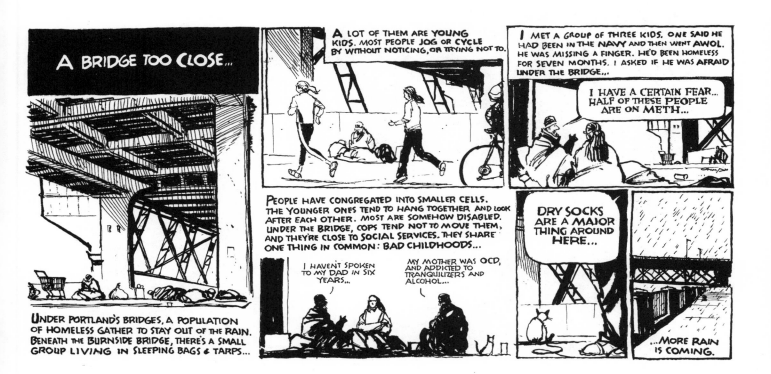

JACK OHMAN

Editorial Cartoonist
The Oregonian

Born in 1960 in St. Paul, Minnesota; attended the University of Minnesota; graduated in the honors program from Portland State University; at age 19 was the youngest-ever syndicated cartoonist; editorial cartoonist for the *Columbus Dispatch*, 1981-82, the *Detroit Free Press*, 1982-83, and *The Oregonian*, 1983 to the present; recipient of the Society of Professional Journalists Mark of Excellence Award, 1980, the Thomas Nast Award, 1995, the National Headliner Award, 2002, and the Robert F. Kennedy Journalism Award, 2009; author of nine books; cartoons syndicated by Tribune Media Services.

2010 THOMAS NAST AWARD

NATE BEELER

Editorial Cartoonist
Washington Examiner

Born in Columbus, Ohio, in 1980; earned degree in journalism at American University in 2002; editorial cartoonist for the *Washington Examiner* since 2005; past winner of the Berryman Award and the Golden Spike Award for cartooning; as a student, won the three major college cartooning awards; work syndicated by Cagle Cartoons in more than 800 publications.

2009 SCRIPPS HOWARD AWARD

(Awarded in 2010)

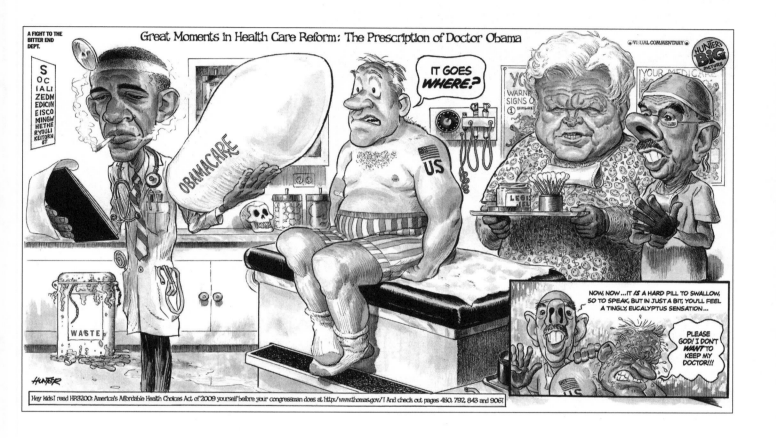

ALEXANDER HUNTER

Editorial Cartoonist
The Washington Times

Born in Long Beach, California, in 1960; received art education at an early age from his parents, who were gifted artists; for the past 28 years has been a staff member of *The Washington Times* where he has served as an illustrator, political cartoonist, graphic designer, as well as art director for almost every section of the newspaper; currently art director for the *Times'* daily Commentary section; winner of more than two dozen awards for excellence.

2009 JOHN FISCHETTI AWARD
(Awarded in 2010)

STEVE BREEN

Editorial Cartoonist
San Diego Union-Tribune

Born in Los Angeles in 1970; attended the University of California at Riverside; editorial cartoonist for the *San Diego Union-Tribune* since 2001; two-time winner of the Pulitzer Prize for editorial cartooning, in 1998 and 2009; also received the 2007 Berryman Award, the 2009 Thomas Nast Award, and the 2009 National Headliner Award for editorial cartooning; writes and illustrates picture books, among them *Stick* (2007), *Violet the Pilot* (2008), and *The Secret of Santa's Island* (2009); cartoons distributed nationally by Creators News Service.

2010 HERBLOCK AWARD

MATT WUERKER

Editorial Cartoonist
Politico

An editorial cartoonist for more than 25 years; was among a group who founded newspaper/web site *Politico* in 2006; creates cartoons, caricatures, and animations for print and web; was twice a finalist for the Pulitzer Prize for editorial cartooning.

BEST
EDITORIAL
CARTOONS
OF THE YEAR

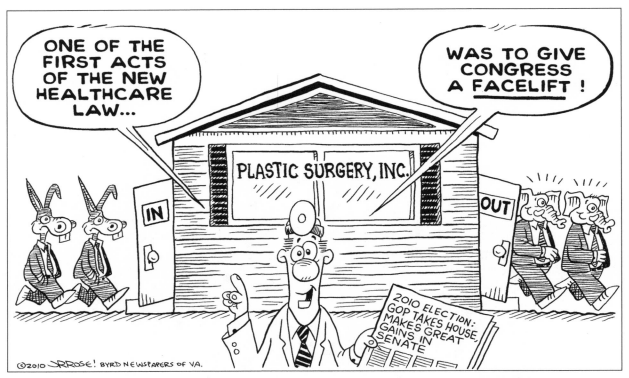

J.R ROSE
Courtesy Byrd Newspapers of Va.

JOHN SHERFFIUS
Courtesy Boulder Camera

The Midterm Election

Riding a wave of voter discontent over deficit spending, runaway government, and disappearing jobs, the Republicans recaptured control of the U.S. House of Representatives in the November midterm election.

The stunning victory in the House, however, was tempered somewhat by the GOP's failure to win control of the Senate. When the dust had settled, the Republican net increase in the House was more than 60 seats, the largest midterm election gain since 1948.

In assessing the election results, President Obama blamed the debacle on the economy. "People are frustrated," he said. "They're deeply frustrated with the pace of our economic recovery."

Senate Minority Leader Mitch McConnell, however, saw the election as "a referendum" on Obama's policies, and he cautioned: "Choosing [to support] the President over your constituency is not a good strategy."

Republican Rep. John Boehner, in line to become Speaker of the House, said, "I think it's pretty clear that the Obama-Pelosi agenda is being rejected by the American people."

Compounding the Democrats' woes, the Republicans added to their governorships and won substantial increases in state legislative seats.

JOSEPH LICCAR
Courtesy Gatehouse Media

STEVE BREEN
Courtesy San Diego Union-Tribune

DAVID HORSEY
Courtesy Hearst Newspapers

The Obama Administration

The Obama Administration continued its runaway spending, lifting the national debt to more than $13 trillion. But in spite of the outpouring of money, the nation's economy remained sluggish, with unemployment stalled above 9 percent. The president's approval rating fell to around 40 percent in some polls.

President Obama publicly scolded the U.S. Supreme Court for its ruling allowing corporations to make political contributions. He drew widespread criticism for what was perceived as a slow response to the massive BP oil spill in the Gulf of Mexico.

Often blaming President Bush for the nation's economic woes, Obama occasionally showed signs of agreement with his predecessor. He based his strategy in Afghanistan on Bush's counterinsurgency tactics in Iraq.

NASA administrator Charles Bolden raised a ruckus when he declared that the foremost mission of the space agency was to reach out to the Muslim world and "help them feel good" about their historic scientific contributions. Department of Agriculture employee Shirley Sherrod was fired after an edited video seemed to show she had refused to assist a white farmer because of race. When the full speech was shown she was vindicated.

SCOTT STANTIS
Courtesy Chicago Tribune

WALT HANDELSMAN
Courtesy Newsday

JOE HELLER
Courtesy Green Bay Press

TIM HARTMAN
Courtesy Beaver County Times (Pa.)

JEFF STAHLER
Courtesy Columbus Dispatch

DAVID BROWN
Courtesy David G. Brown Studios

SCOTT STANTIS
Courtesy Chicago Tribune

ADAM ZYGLIS
Courtesy Buffalo News

JERRY BREEN
Courtesy newbreen.com

STEVE NEASE
Courtesy Toronto Sun (Can.)

ADAM ZYGLIS
Courtesy Buffalo News

JOSEPH LICCAR
Courtesy Gatehouse Media

WAYNE STROOT
Courtesy Hastings Tribune

THE WILDERNESS EXPERIENCE

JAKE FULLER
Courtesy Artizans.com

BOB GORRELL
Courtesy Creators.com

CHARLIE DANIEL
Courtesy Knoxville News-Sentinel

JAKE FULLER
Courtesy Artizans.com

WARTIME PRESIDENTS

MIKE PETERS
Courtesy Dayton Daily News/
    King Features

STEVE BREEN
Courtesy San Diego Union-Tribune

ED HALL
Courtesy Baker County Press (Fla.)

BILL GARNER
Courtesy Creators.com

BOB LANG
Courtesy Rightoons.com

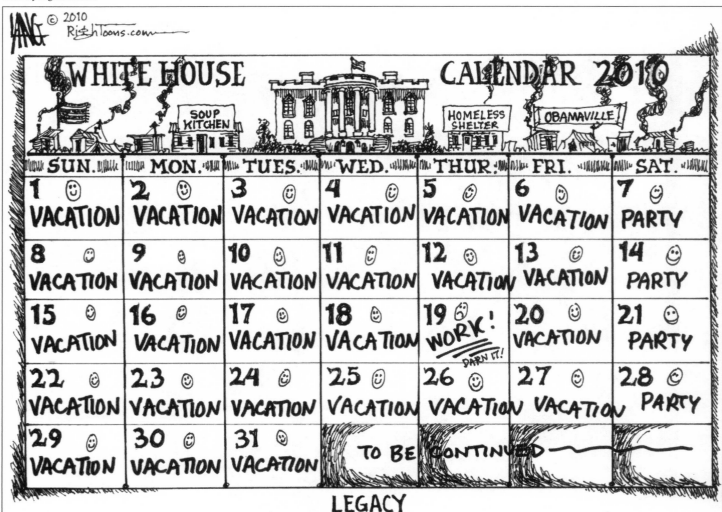

HEAR ME, OH GOD OF EUROPEAN STYLE STATIST GOVERNMENT. GRANT YOUR SERVANT, OBAMA THE MAGNIFICENT, THE POWER TO CLEANSE THESE WATERS...ONCE THE PEOPLE HAVE RENOUNCED THE EVIL OF OFF-SHORE DRILLING.

STEPHEN RUSTAD
Courtesy Steve Rustad Blogs

NICK ANDERSON
Courtesy Houston Chronicle

INCONCLUSIVE, EQUIVOCAL, AMBIGUOUS, INDEFINITE, TENUOUS, UNSETTLED, INDETERMINATE, DUBIOUS, UNPREDICTABLE, ERRATIC, UNCERTAIN, PRECARIOUS STASIS ACCOMPLISHED

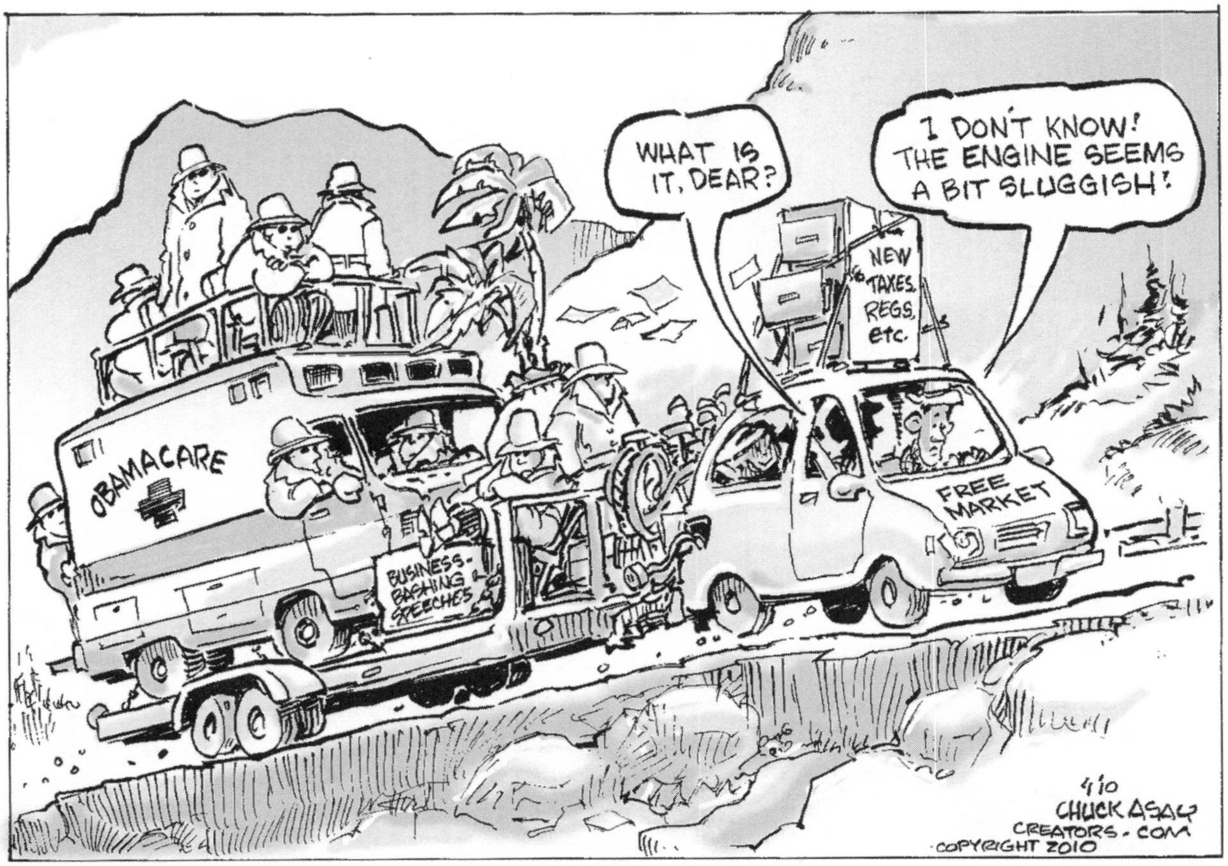
WHAT IS IT, DEAR?
I DON'T KNOW! THE ENGINE SEEMS A BIT SLUGGISH!
NEW TAXES, REGS, etc.
OBAMACARE
BUSINESS-BASHING SPEECHES
FREE MARKET
4/10
CHUCK ASAY
CREATORS.COM
COPYRIGHT 2010

CHUCK ASAY
Courtesy Creators.com

JERRY BARNETT
Courtesy Boonville Standard (Ind.)

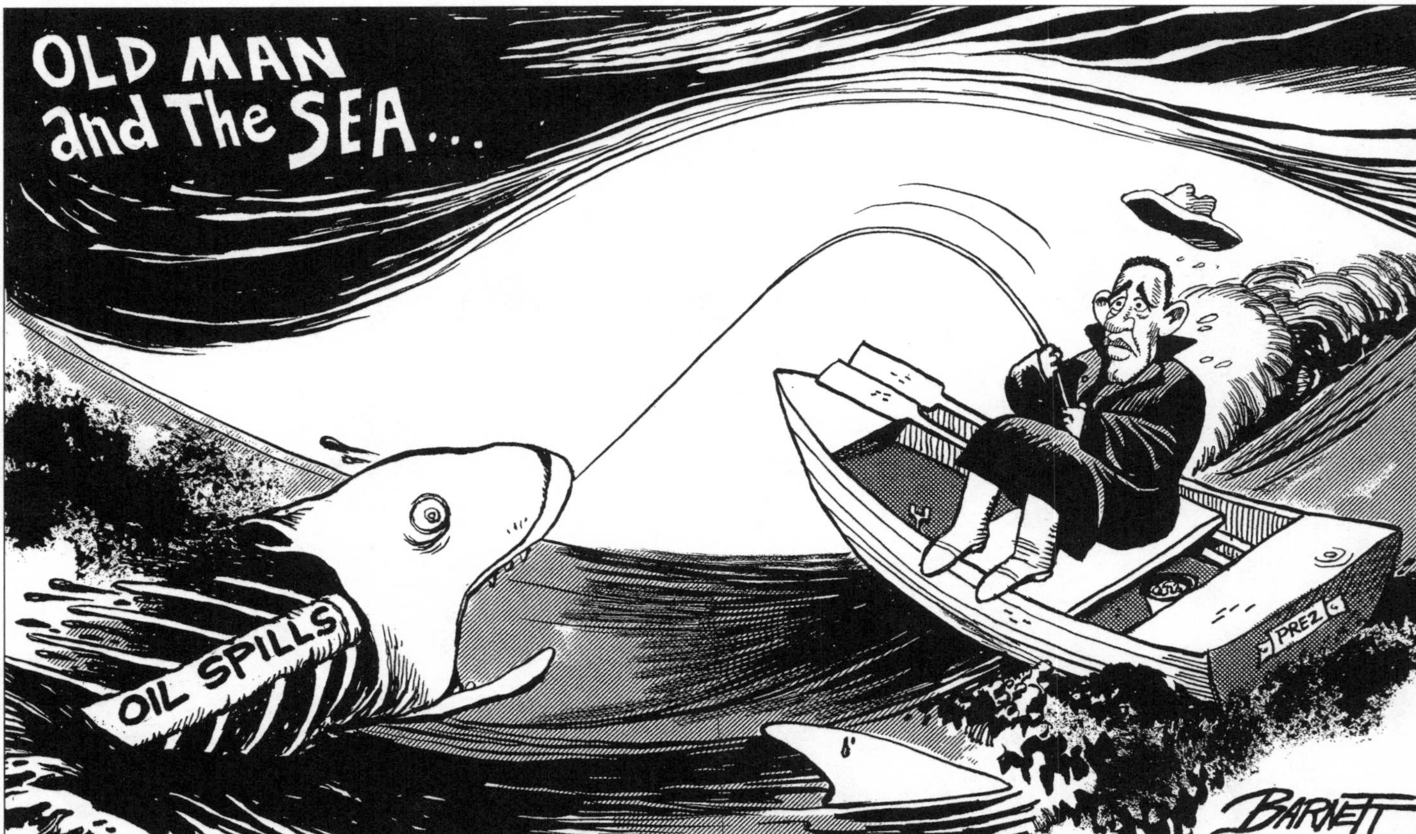
OLD MAN and The SEA...
OIL SPILLS
PREZ
BARNETT

MATT WUERKER
Courtesy Politico

JERRY BARNETT
Courtesy Boonville Standard (Ind.)

MICHAEL RAMIREZ
Courtesy Investor's Business Daily

DICK LOCHER
Courtesy Chicago Tribune Media Services

JUSTIN DEFREITAS
Courtesy Berkeley Daily Planet

GLENN FODEN
Courtesy Artizans.com

JOHN TREVER
Courtesy Albuquerque Journal

MIKE KEEFE
Courtesy Denver Post

Politics

Washington-style politics seemed to grow less popular with the American people during the year. A Rasmussen poll showed that only 16 percent felt that Congress was doing a good job and that 88 percent believed congressmen were primarily looking out for themselves. A Gallup Poll showed Democrats with a slightly higher approval rating than Republicans.

The White House employed former President Bill Clinton as an intermediary to try to persuade Rep. Joe Sestak to drop out of the Senate primary. There were various allegations of questionable job offers involved, but the White House insisted there was nothing improper.

Non-elected Washington power mongers such as administration czars and lobbyists continued to wield the real clout. Midterm elections focused on whether to extend the Bush tax cuts. Democrats wanted to extend the cuts for Americans making less than $250,000 a year but Republicans pushed for cuts for everybody.

Tea Party Senate candidate Rand Paul won a decisive victory in the Kentucky Republican primary. Two prominent Democrats, Rep. Charles Rangel and Rep. Maxine Waters, faced ethics charges, and a salmonella outbreak in eggs led to congressional hearings.

RANDY BISH
Courtesy Pittsburgh Tribune-Review

SCOTT COFFMAN
Courtesy Louisville Courier-Journal

STEPHEN TEMPLETON
Courtesy Flathead Beacon.com

STEVE MCBRIDE
Courtesy Independence Reporter (Kan.)

DANIEL FITZGERALD
Courtesy Louisville Courier-Journal

JEFF STAHLER
Courtesy Columbus Dispatch

ED GAMBLE
Courtesy Florida Times-Union

RICK KOLLINGER
Courtesy Star-Democrat (Md.)

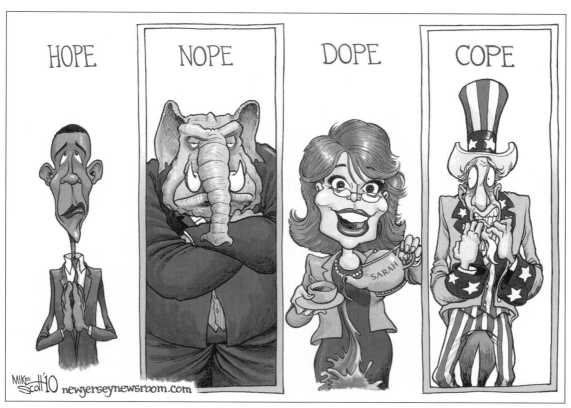

MIKE SCOTT
Courtesy New Jersey Newsroom.com

PAUL FELL
Courtesy Artizans Syndicate

JEFF HICKMAN
Courtesy Reno Gazette-Journal

ROBERT ARIAIL
Courtesy ROBERTARIAIL.COM

ED STEIN
Courtesy EDSTEININK.COM

STEVEN LAIT
Courtesy Oakland Tribune

CLAY BENNETT
Courtesy Chattanooga Times-Free Press

'I'll bet HIS wish comes true.'

TERRY WISE
Courtesy Ratland.com

J.R ROSE
Courtesy Byrd Newspapers of Va.

TOM STIGLICH
Courtesy TOMSTIGLICH.COM

LINDA BOILEAU
Courtesy Frankfort State Journal

JEFF DARCY
Courtesy The Plain Dealer (Oh.)

JIMMY MARGULIES
Courtesy JimMarg.com

DAVID HITCH
Courtesy Worcester Telegram & Gazette (Mass.)

MIKE GEMPELER
Courtesy Lee's Summit Journal (Mo.)

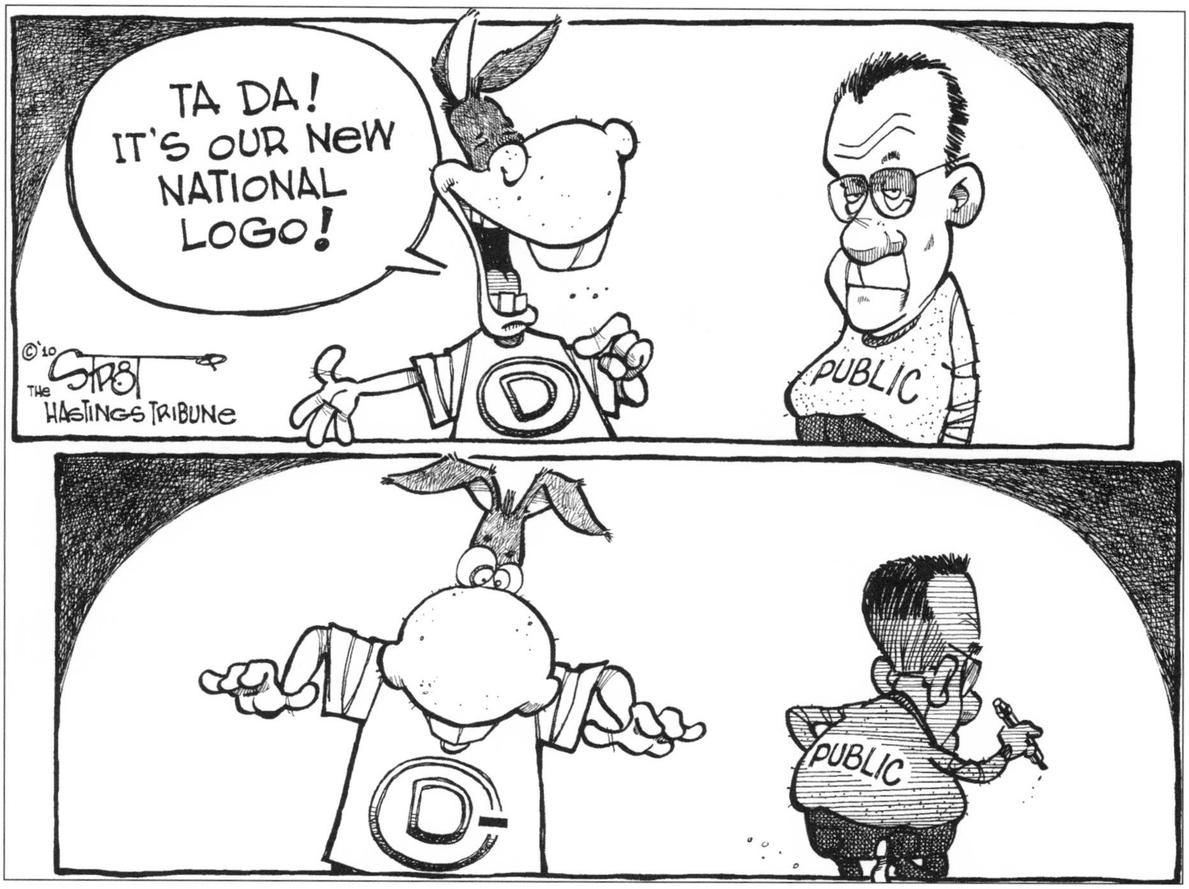
TA DA! IT'S OUR NEW NATIONAL LOGO!
©'10 STROOT
The HASTINGS TRIBUNE
PUBLIC
D
PUBLIC
D-

WAYNE STROOT
Courtesy Hastings Tribune

JOHN AUCHTER
Courtesy Grand Rapids Press

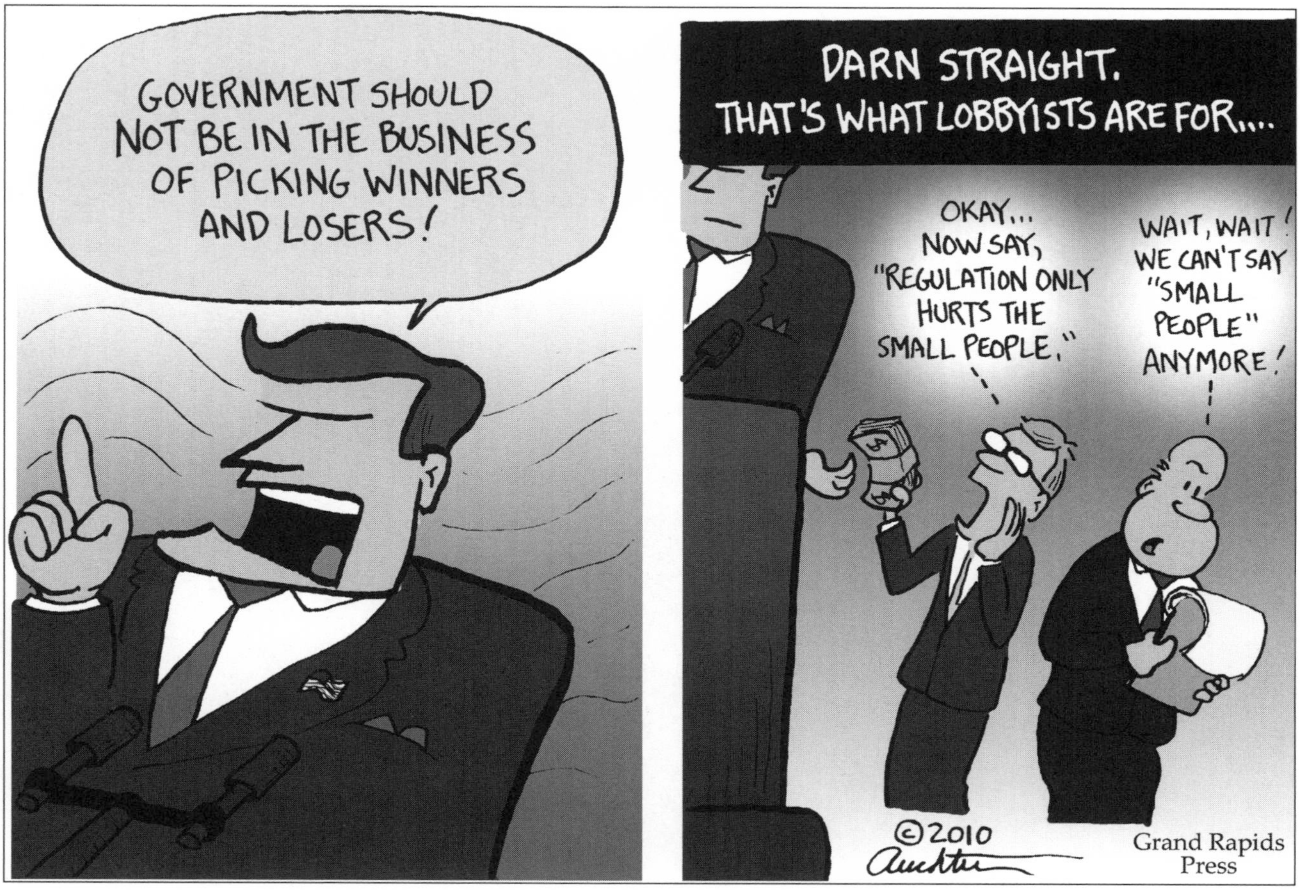
GOVERNMENT SHOULD NOT BE IN THE BUSINESS OF PICKING WINNERS AND LOSERS!
DARN STRAIGHT. THAT'S WHAT LOBBYISTS ARE FOR....
OKAY... NOW SAY, "REGULATION ONLY HURTS THE SMALL PEOPLE."
WAIT, WAIT! WE CAN'T SAY "SMALL PEOPLE" ANYMORE!
©2010
Auchter
Grand Rapids Press

CLAY BENNETT
Courtesy Chattanooga Times-Free Press

TIM JACKSON
Courtesy Chicago Defender

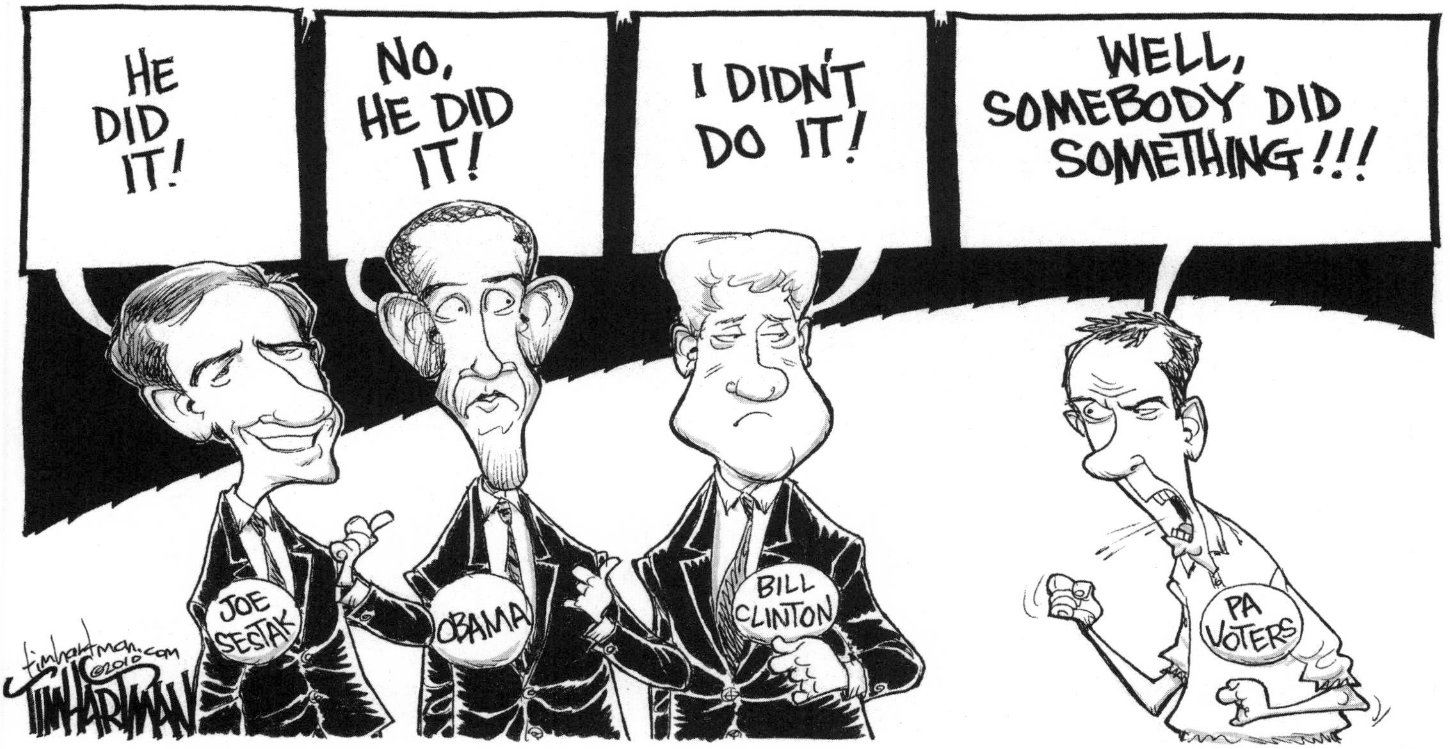
HE DID IT!
NO, HE DID IT!
I DIDN'T DO IT!
WELL, SOMEBODY DID SOMETHING!!!
JOE SESTAK
OBAMA
BILL CLINTON
PA VOTERS
timhartman.com ©2010
TIM HARTMAN

TIM HARTMAN
Courtesy Beaver County Times (Pa.)

SEEING NO BOUNCE ON HEALTH CARE, THE DEMS NOW FOCUS ON IMMIGRATION REFORM

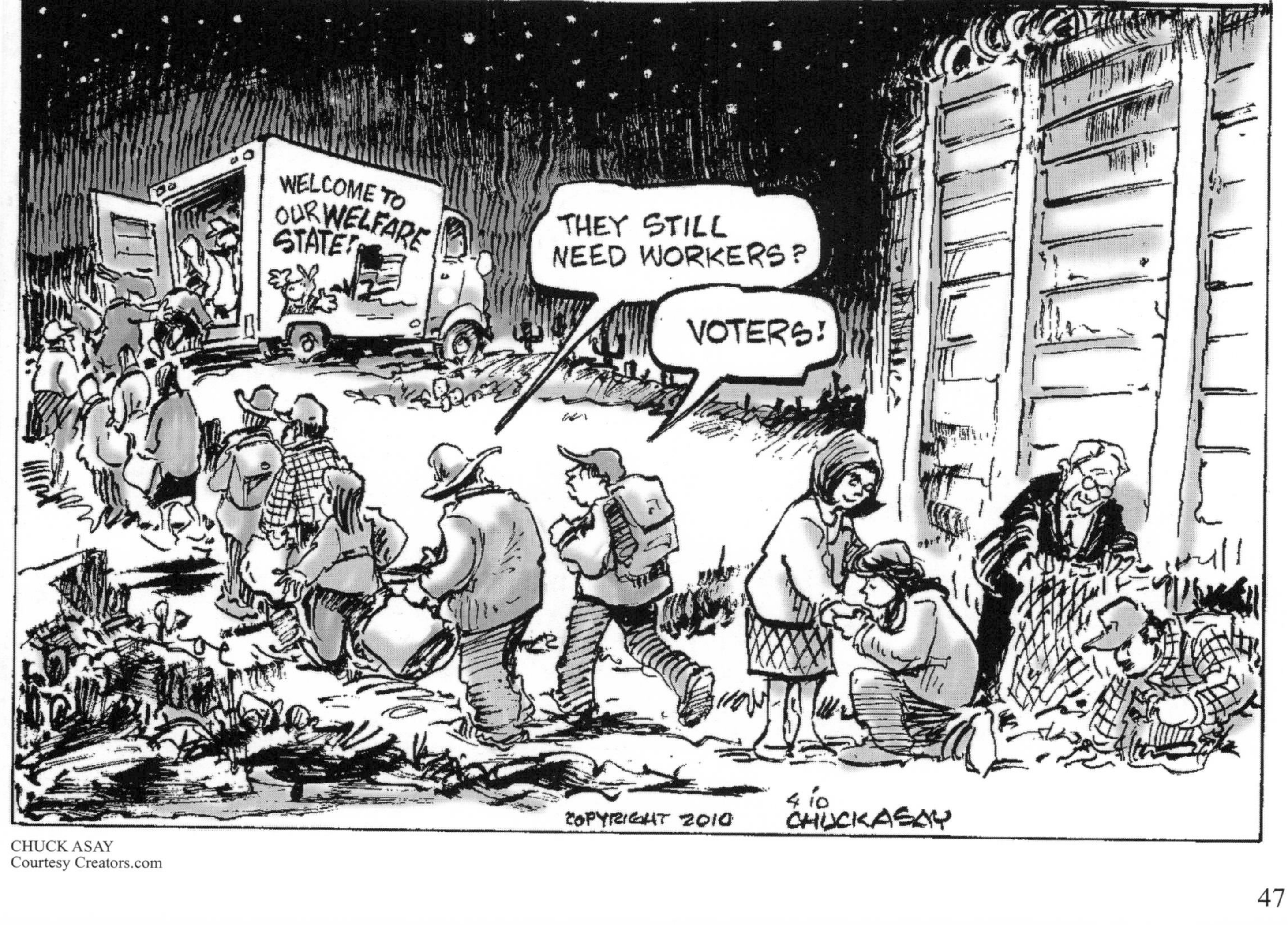
WELCOME TO OUR WELFARE STATE!
THEY STILL NEED WORKERS?
VOTERS!
COPYRIGHT 2010
4 10
CHUCKASAY

CHUCK ASAY
Courtesy Creators.com

ED FISCHER
Courtesy Ed Fischer

ED HALL
Courtesy Baker County Press (Fla.)

NEIL GRAHAME
Courtesy Spencer Newspapers

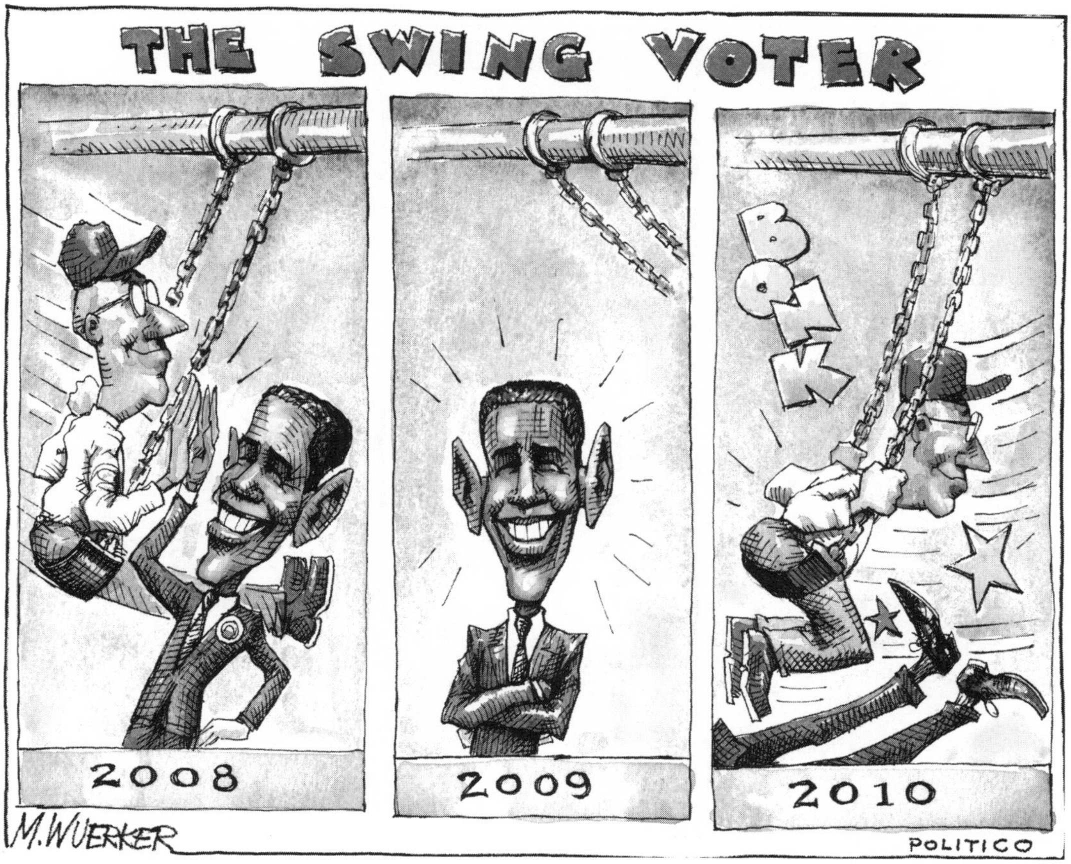
THE SWING VOTER
2008
2009
BONK
2010
M.WUERKER
POLITICO

JOHN AUCHTER
Courtesy Grand Rapids Press

MATT WUERKER
Courtesy Politico

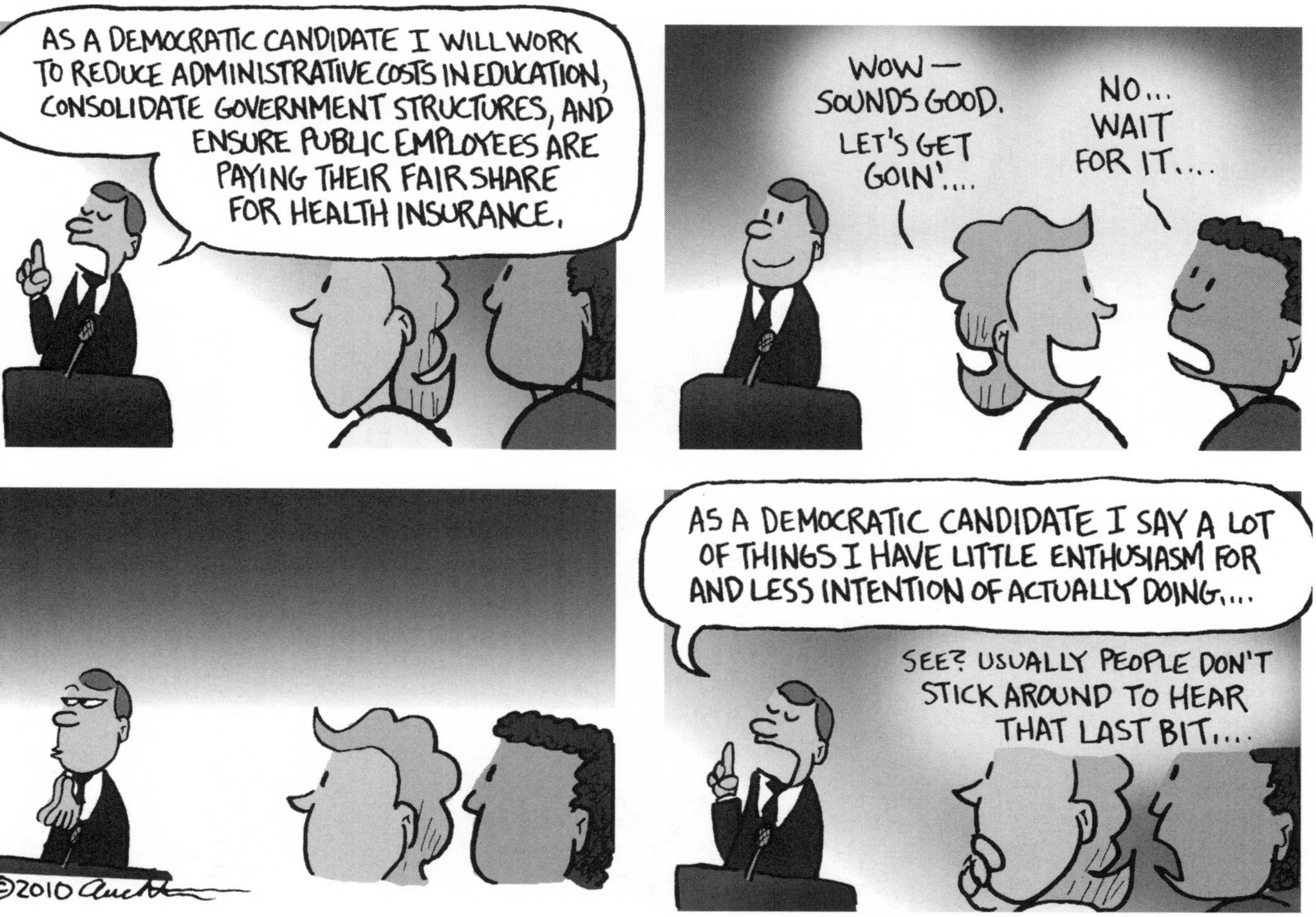
AS A DEMOCRATIC CANDIDATE I WILL WORK TO REDUCE ADMINISTRATIVE COSTS IN EDUCATION, CONSOLIDATE GOVERNMENT STRUCTURES, AND ENSURE PUBLIC EMPLOYEES ARE PAYING THEIR FAIR SHARE FOR HEALTH INSURANCE.
WOW — SOUNDS GOOD. LET'S GET GOIN'....
NO... WAIT FOR IT....
AS A DEMOCRATIC CANDIDATE I SAY A LOT OF THINGS I HAVE LITTLE ENTHUSIASM FOR AND LESS INTENTION OF ACTUALLY DOING....
SEE? USUALLY PEOPLE DON'T STICK AROUND TO HEAR THAT LAST BIT....
©2010 Auchter

MILT PRIGGEE
Courtesy miltpriggee.com

GLENN FODEN
Courtesy Artizans.com

Spending

Out of control federal spending in 2010 threatened to push the U.S. further into recession and damage the nation's economy for generations to come. Many believe the U.S. is following the same path that has led Greece to violence and financial ruin. Spending programs promoted by President Obama raised the national debt to $13 trillion, while the $787 billion stimulus package seemed to have had little effect on unemployment.

Spending and deficits continued to grow at a pace not seen since World War II. In 2010, Washington spent $30,543 per household—some $5,000 more than just two years earlier. While some of this spending is a temporary result of the recession, Obama's latest budget would replace this temporary spending with permanent new programs. Consequently, by 2020, a time of presumed peace and prosperity, Washington would still spend nearly $36,000 per household.

Some states, most notably California, have joined the spending spree and now must contend with severely strained, deficit-laden budgets.

JUSTIN DEFREITAS
Courtesy Berkeley Daily Planet

STEVE KELLEY
Courtesy Times-Picayune (La.)

GARY VARVEL
Courtesy Indianapolis Star

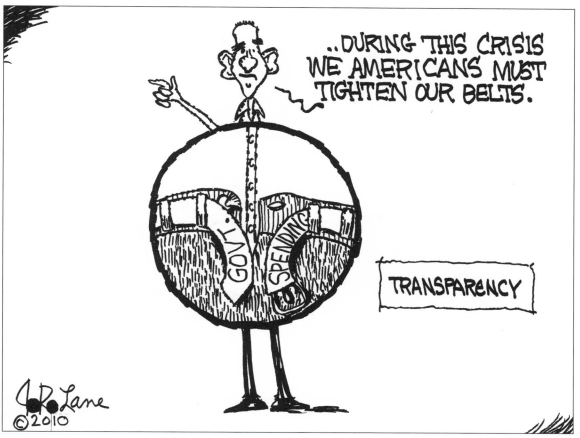

JOE R. LANE
Courtesy Joe R. Lane

NATE BEELER
Courtesy Washington Examiner

MICHAEL OSBUN
Courtesy Tribune Media Services

JIM DYKE
Courtesy Jefferson City News-Tribune (Mo.)

DENNIS GALVEZ
Courtesy Philippine News

LISA BENSON
Courtesy Washington Post Writers Group

DAVE SATTLER
Courtesy Lafayette Journal & Courier (Ind.)

WILLIAM WARREN
Courtesy Liberty Features Syndicate

JOHN TREVER
Courtesy Albuquerque Journal

CHARLIE DANIEL
Courtesy Knoxville News-Sentinel

DICK WALLMEYER
Courtesy Long Beach Press-Telegram

STEVE KELLEY
Courtesy Times-Picayune (La.)

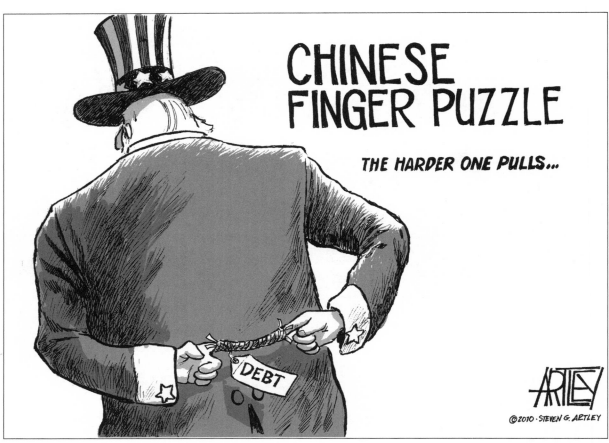

JEFF PARKER
Courtesy Florida Today

STEVE ARTLEY
Courtesy artleytoons.com

JIM DYKE
Courtesy Jefferson City News-Tribune (Mo.)

DICK WALLMEYER
Courtesy Long Beach Press-Telegram

GARY VARVEL
Courtesy Indianapolis Star

The Economy

At year's end, the national debt stood at more than $13 trillion. That debt has risen by more than $500 billion every year since fiscal 2003, with increases of $1 trillion in 2008 and $1.9 trillion in 2009.

Congress passed a $787 billion economic stimulus package aimed at creating jobs and helping the nation recover from the recession caused by the collapse of financial institutions and the housing market in 2008. The government says the stimulus created at least 700,000 jobs, but there are high-profile dissenters and critics. Former Fed Chairman Alan Greenspan declared that stimulus efforts had fallen short of expectations and that the government now needs to get out of the way "and allow the economy to heal itself."

Despite the stimulus spending, job growth remained weak, with unemployment hovering just below 10 percent—a 27-year high. California's economy faced daunting problems with high unemployment, mortgage turmoil, and soaring home foreclosures.

TAYLOR JONES
Courtesy Cagle Cartoons

ED STEIN
Courtesy EDSTEININK.COM

DAVE SATTLER
Courtesy Lafayette Journal & Courier (Ind.)

WALT HANDELSMAN
Courtesy Newsday

CHRIS BRITT
Courtesy State Journal-Register (Ill.)

MICHAEL RAMIREZ
Courtesy Investor's Business Daily

DARREL AKERS
Courtesy Vacaville Reporter (Calif.)

ANNETTE BALESTERI
Courtesy Antioch News (Calif.)

MIKE KONOPACKI
Courtesy Madison Capital Times (Wisc.)

PHIL HANDS
Courtesy Wisconsin State Journal

MIKE SPICER
Courtesy Mike Spicer

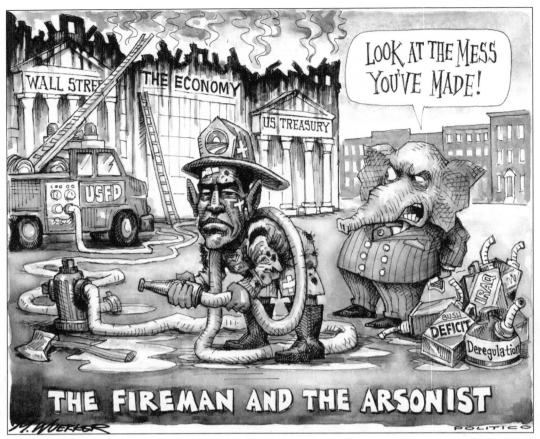

JESSE SPRINGER
Courtesy Eugene Register-Guard

MATT WUERKER
Courtesy Politico

GLENN FODEN
Courtesy Artizans.com

CHRIS BRITT
Courtesy State Journal-Register (Ill.)

MIKE SCOTT
Courtesy New Jersey Newsroom.com

JOSEPH HOFFECKER
Courtesy American City Business Journals

JESSE SPRINGER
Courtesy Eugene Register-Guard

JEFF PARKER
Courtesy Florida Today

JEFF DANZIGER
Courtesy NYTS/CWS

ROBERT UNELL
Courtesy Kansas City Star

WILLIAM WARREN
Courtesy Liberty Features Syndicate

70

MIKE BECKOM
Courtesy Index-Journal (S.C.)

ANNETTE BALESTERI
Courtesy Antioch News (Calif.)

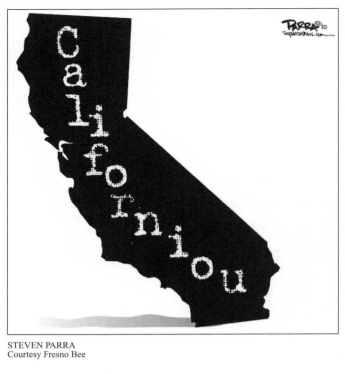

STEVEN PARRA
Courtesy Fresno Bee

STEVE NEASE
Courtesy Toronto Sun (Can.)

KARL WIMER
Courtesy Denver Business Journal

MICHAEL RAMIREZ
Courtesy Investor's Business Daily

CHRIS BRITT
Courtesy State Journal-Register (Ill.)

DICK LOCHER
Courtesy Chicago Tribune Media Services

MILT PRIGGEE
Courtesy miltpriggee.com

MARTY RISKIN
Courtesy Penspeak

JEFF PARKER
Courtesy Florida Today

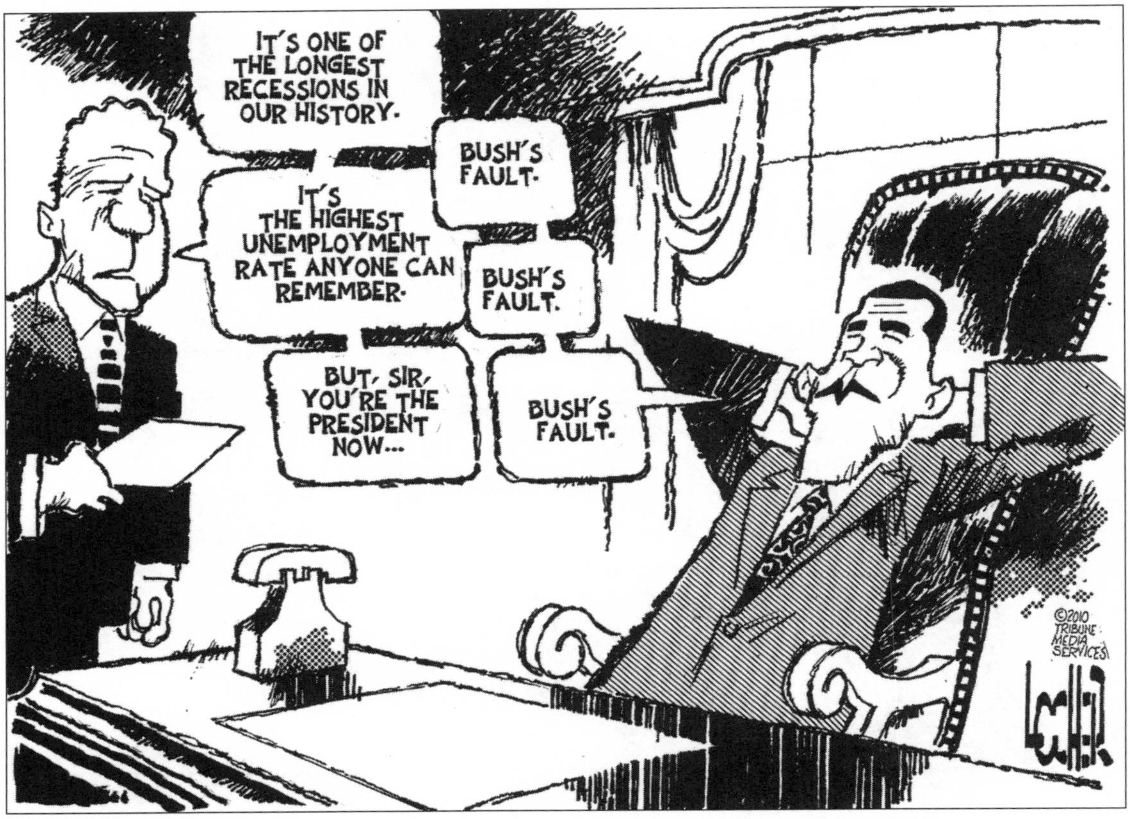
IT'S ONE OF THE LONGEST RECESSIONS IN OUR HISTORY.
BUSH'S FAULT.
IT'S THE HIGHEST UNEMPLOYMENT RATE ANYONE CAN REMEMBER.
BUSH'S FAULT.
BUT, SIR, YOU'RE THE PRESIDENT NOW...
BUSH'S FAULT.
©2010 TRIBUNE MEDIA SERVICES
LOCHER

DICK LOCHER
Courtesy Chicago Tribune Media Services

CHRIS BRITT
Courtesy State Journal-Register (Ill.)

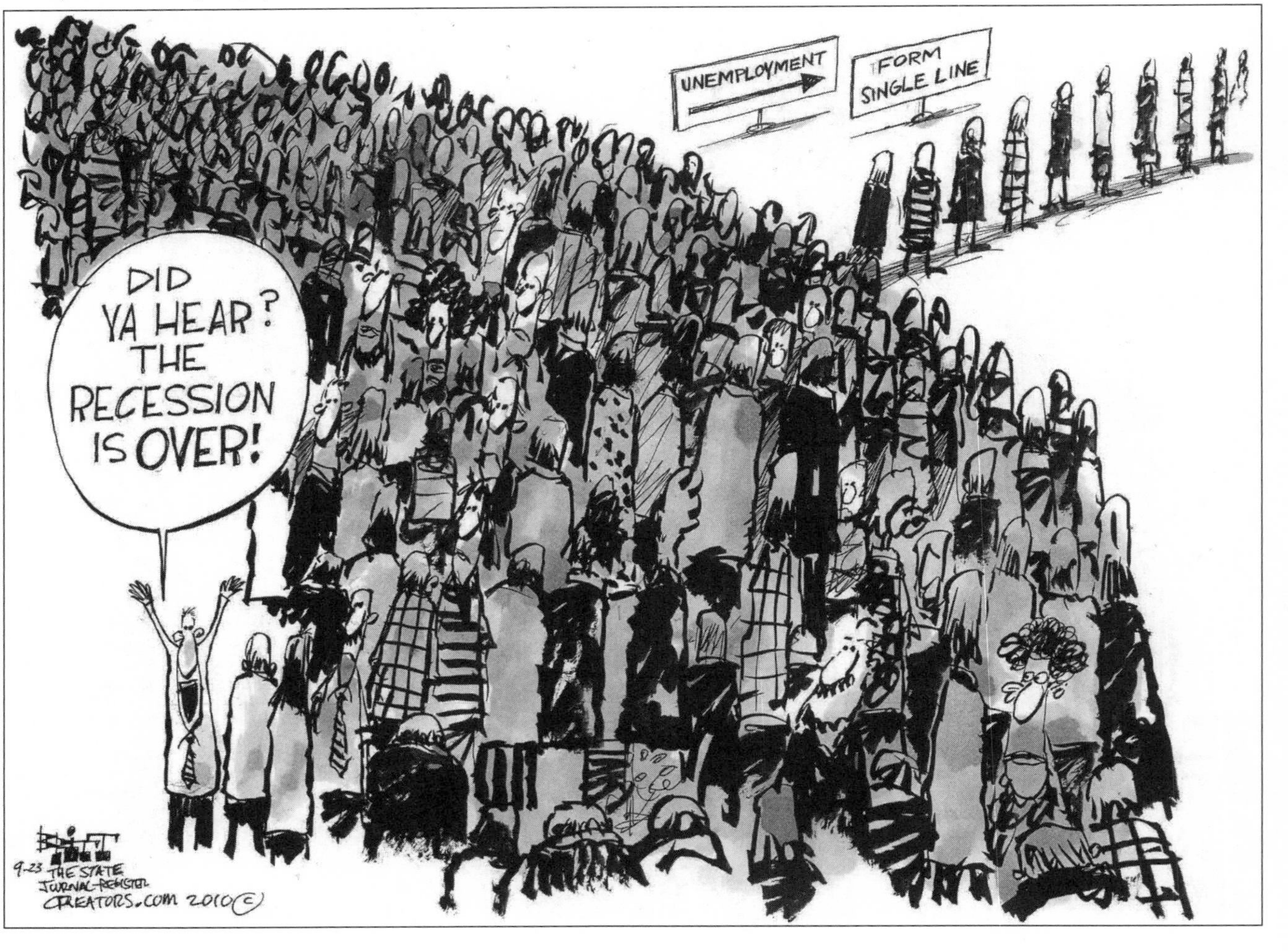
UNEMPLOYMENT
FORM SINGLE LINE
DID YA HEAR? THE RECESSION IS OVER!
BRITT
9-23 THE STATE JOURNAL-REGISTER
CREATORS.COM 2010©

The Tea Party

The Tea Party movement, born in 2009 as a protest against ever-higher taxes and government spending, came into its own in 2010. Tea Partiers flexed their political muscle in a number of elections, beginning with the surprising sweep into office of Republican Sen. Scott Brown in Massachusetts.

Rand Paul, son of Republican Rep. Ron Paul of Texas, won the GOP's Super Tuesday primary in Kentucky, easily defeating the Republican establishment candidate. The Tea Party movement also upset the GOP hierarchy in numerous other states, including Delaware and Nevada.

The typical Tea Party member appeared to be an ordinary citizen who had never taken an active role in politics before. The movement has taken the political world by storm and is clearly a force to be reckoned with.

A leader in the fight against construction of the Ground Zero mosque was tossed out of the National Tea Party Federation for what many perceived as a racist blog. The federation claimed to represent 85 Tea Party groups. The NAACP called on Tea Party leaders to repudiate racism in their ranks.

STEVE GREENBERG
Courtesy Ventura County Reporter (Calif.)

JIM HUNT
Courtesy Charlotte Post

JOSEPH RANK
Courtesy krankyscartoons.com

JESSE SPRINGER
Courtesy Eugene Register-Guard

PAUL BERGE
Courtesy Racine Post (Wisc.)

MIKE MARLAND
Courtesy Concord Monito

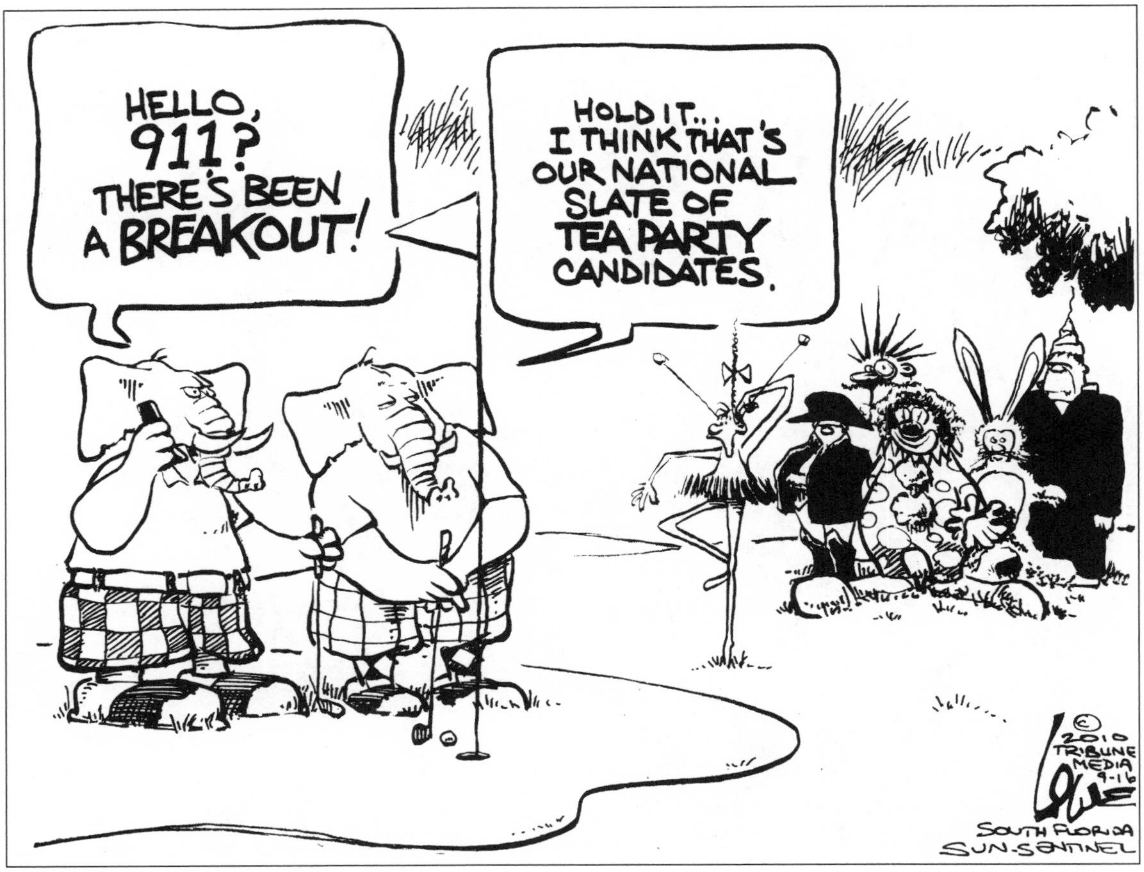
HELLO, 911? THERE'S BEEN A BREAKOUT!
HOLD IT... I THINK THAT'S OUR NATIONAL SLATE OF TEA PARTY CANDIDATES.
© 2010 TRIBUNE MEDIA 9-16
LOWE
SOUTH FLORIDA SUN-SENTINEL

CHAN LOWE
Courtesy South Florida Sun-Sentinel/
Tribune Media Services

BRUCE PLANTE
Courtesy Tulsa World

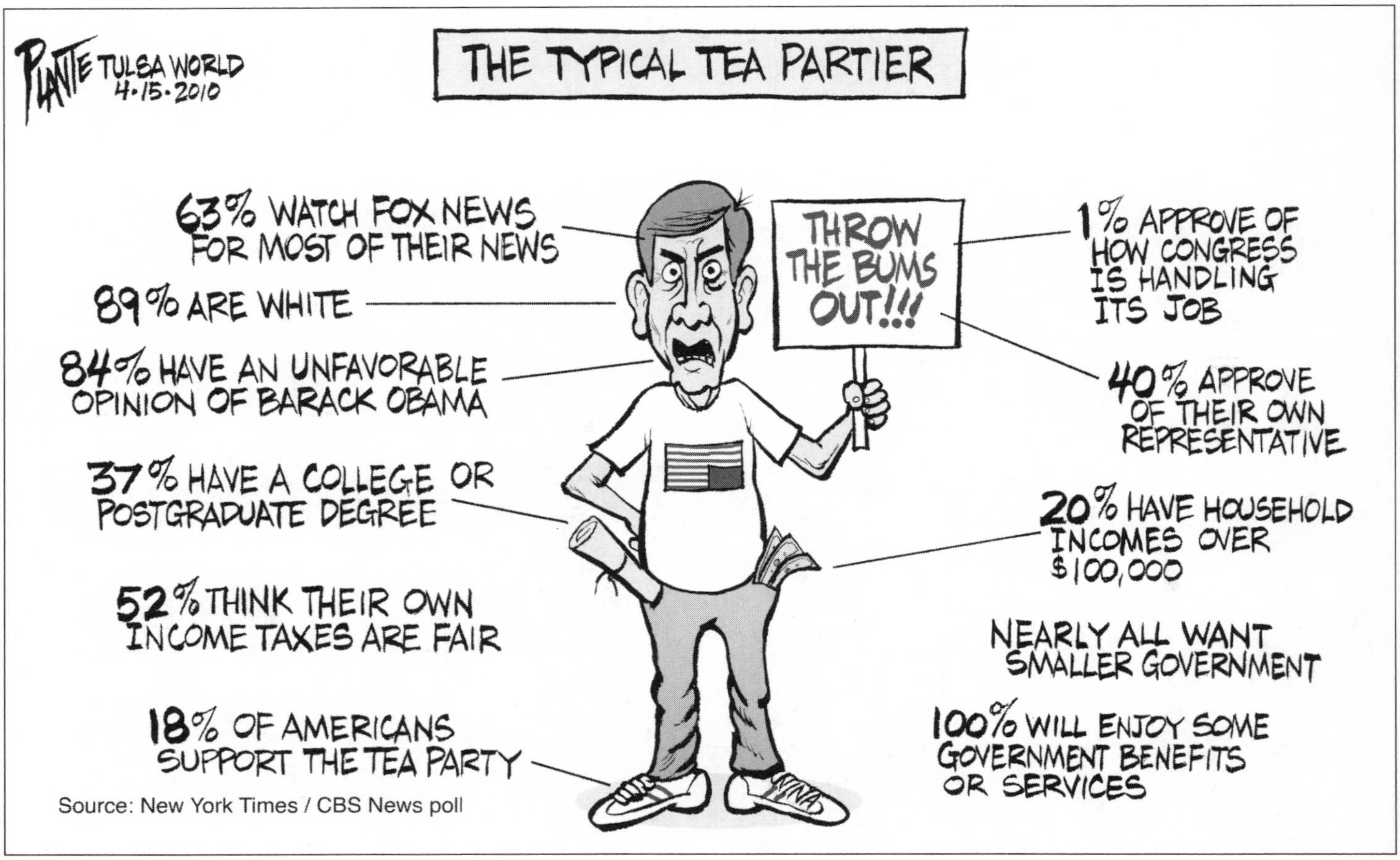
PLANTE TULSA WORLD 4·15·2010
THE TYPICAL TEA PARTIER
63% WATCH FOX NEWS FOR MOST OF THEIR NEWS
89% ARE WHITE
84% HAVE AN UNFAVORABLE OPINION OF BARACK OBAMA
37% HAVE A COLLEGE OR POSTGRADUATE DEGREE
52% THINK THEIR OWN INCOME TAXES ARE FAIR
18% OF AMERICANS SUPPORT THE TEA PARTY
THROW THE BUMS OUT!!!
1% APPROVE OF HOW CONGRESS IS HANDLING ITS JOB
40% APPROVE OF THEIR OWN REPRESENTATIVE
20% HAVE HOUSEHOLD INCOMES OVER $100,000
NEARLY ALL WANT SMALLER GOVERNMENT
100% WILL ENJOY SOME GOVERNMENT BENEFITS OR SERVICES
Source: New York Times / CBS News poll

JOSEPH O'MAHONEY
Courtesy The Patriot Ledger

DAVID HITCH
Courtesy Worcester Telegram & Gazette (Mass.)

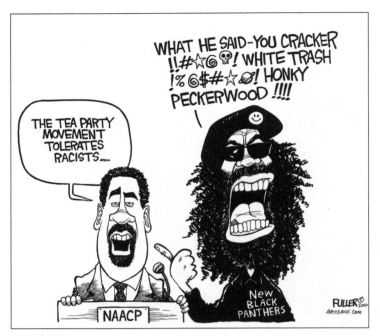

JAKE FULLER
Courtesy Artizans.com

STEPHEN TEMPLETON
Courtesy Flathead Beacon.com

JEFF HICKMAN
Courtesy Reno Gazette-Journal

MATT WUERKER
Courtesy Politico

CHUCK ASAY
Courtesy Creators.com

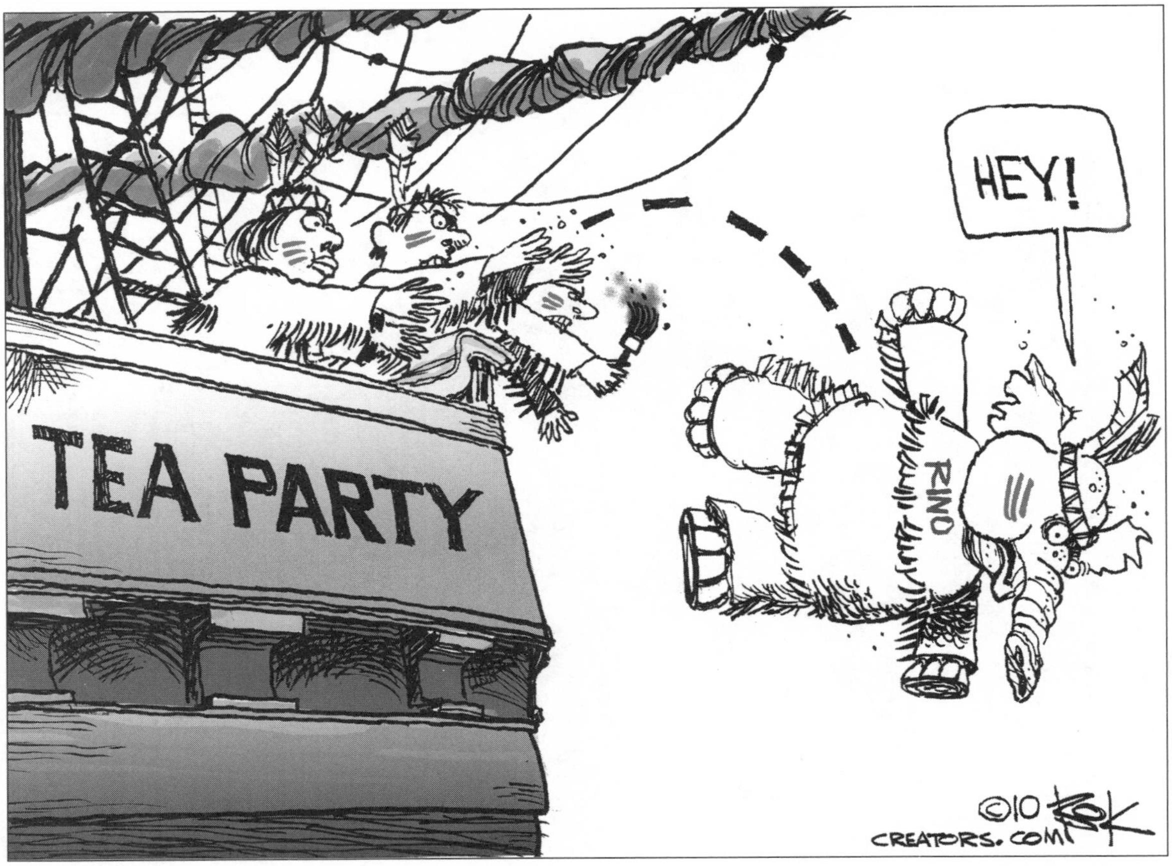
HEY!
TEA PARTY
RINO
©10 BOK
CREATORS.COM

CHIP BOK
Courtesy Creators.com

DICK LOCHER
Courtesy Chicago Tribune Media Services

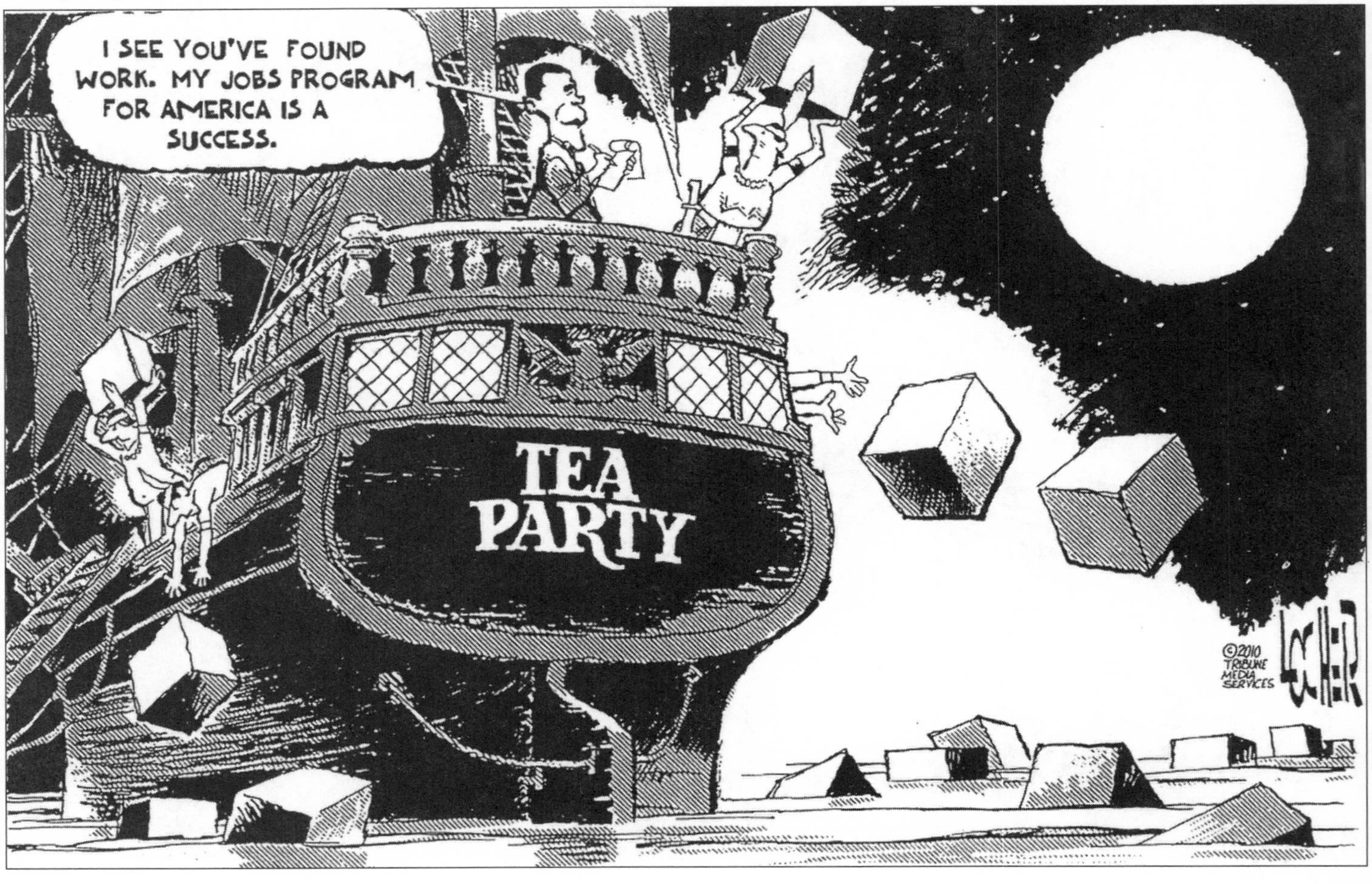
I SEE YOU'VE FOUND WORK. MY JOBS PROGRAM FOR AMERICA IS A SUCCESS.
TEA PARTY
©2010 TRIBUNE MEDIA SERVICES
LOCHER

BOB LANG
Courtesy Rightoons.com

GLENN FODEN
Courtesy Artizans.com

JAKE FULLER
Courtesy Artizans.com

JAY LAMM
Courtesy Franklin Times (N.C.)

STEVE MCBRIDE
Courtesy Independence Reporter (Kan.)

STEPHEN TEMPLETON
Courtesy Flathead Beacon.com

ED GAMBLE
Courtesy Florida Times-Union

87

DANIEL FENECH
Courtesy Heritage Newspapers/
   Journal-Register Co

ELIZABETH BRICQUET
Courtesy Kingsport Times-News

JOEL PETT
Courtesy Lexington Herald-Leader

BOB GORRELL
Courtesy Creators.com

DAVID HORSEY
Courtesy Hearst Newspapers

BARRY HUNAU
Courtesy Jerusalem Post

BOB GORRELL
Courtesy Creators.com

Foreign Affairs

On August 31, the last U.S. combat troops left Iraq, technically ending seven years of armed conflict. U.S. troop levels dropped to just below 50,000 in the move from combat to stability operations. Meanwhile, Afghan President Hamid Karzai increased his efforts to win over members of the Taliban.

China announced efforts to develop a missile designed to be launched from land bases with enough accuracy to penetrate aircraft carrier defenses. A South Korean navy ship was sunk near a disputed border with North Korea, and all signs pointed to the latter as the perpetrator. The North Koreans denied it.

Pakistan was hit by some of the worst flooding in the nation's history, and riots broke out in Greece over the implementation of an austerity program intended to head off the nation's economic collapse. Seven people were arrested in Ireland over an alleged plot to kill a Swedish cartoonist who had depicted the prophet Muhammad in a drawing.

Employees of a Canadian coffee shop at Kandahar airfield in Afghanistan were made eligible to receive overseas service medals.

NICK ANDERSON
Courtesy Houston Chronicle

WAYNE STROOT
Courtesy Hastings Tribune

NATE BEELER
Courtesy Washington Examiner

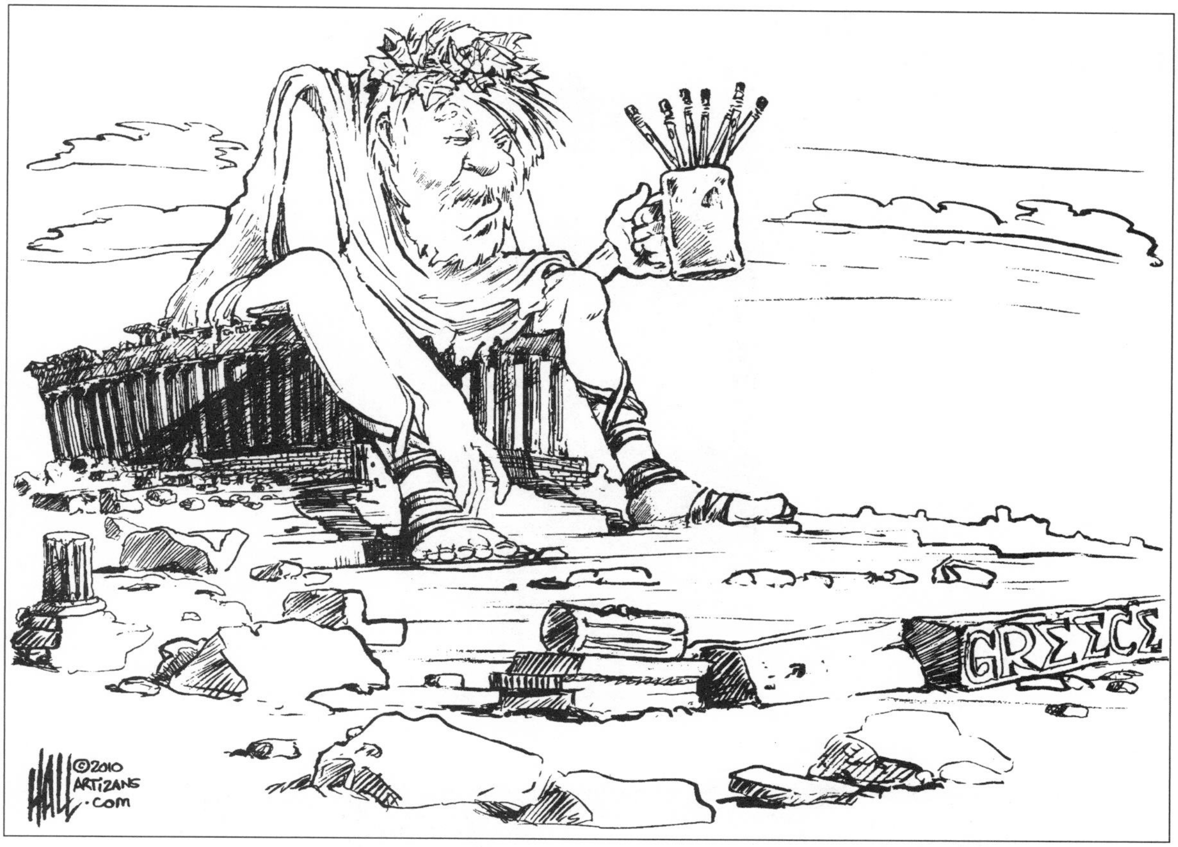
GRΣΣCΣ
©2010 ARTIZANS.com

ED HALL
Courtesy Baker County Press (Fla.)

ROGER SCHILLERSTROM
Courtesy Crain Communications

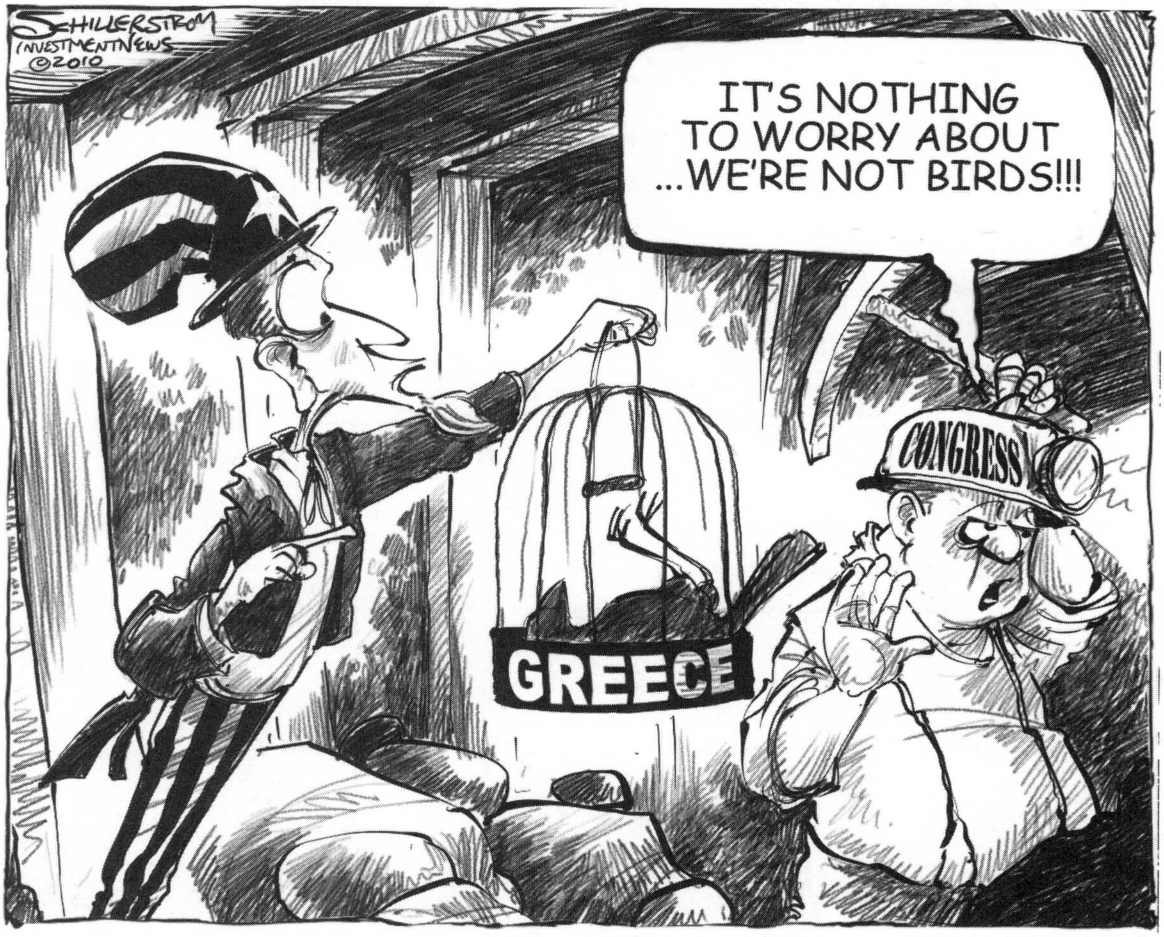
SCHILLERSTROM INVESTMENTNEWS ©2010
IT'S NOTHING TO WORRY ABOUT ...WE'RE NOT BIRDS!!!
CONGRESS
GREECE

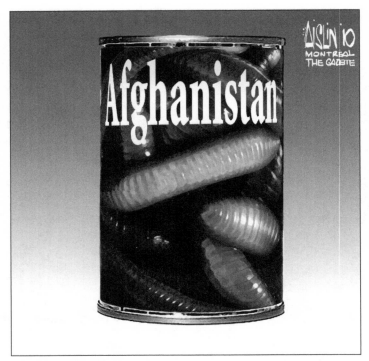

TERRY MOSHER (AISLIN)
Courtesy Montreal Gazette (Can.)

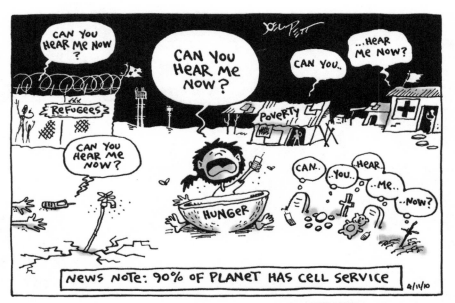

CARL MOORE
Courtesy Creators Syndicate

JOEL PETT
Courtesy Lexington Herald-Leader

LISA BENSON
Courtesy Washington Post Writers Group

MIKE LUCKOVICH
Courtesy Atlanta Journal-Constitution

KEN VEGOTSKY
Courtesy Bucks County Courier Times

MAHMOUD AHMAJINEJAD OF IRAN

FRED SEBASTIAN
Courtesy Artizans Syndicate

MIKE KEEFE
Courtesy Denver Post

JAMES MCCLOSKEY
Courtesy Staunton News-Leader (Va.)

BRUCE MACKINNON
Courtesy Halifax Herald (Can.)

STEVE MCBRIDE
Courtesy Independence Reporter (Kan.)

BOB ENGLEHART
Courtesy Hartford Courant

FRED CURATOLO
Courtesy See Magazine

TIM DOLIGHAN
Courtesy Toronto Sun (Can.)

MARK BAKER
Courtesy Army Times

TERRY MOSHER (AISLIN)
Courtesy Montreal Gazette (Can.)

MIKE SPICER
Courtesy Mike Spicer

TIM DOLIGHAN
Courtesy Toronto Sun (Can.)

BRUCE PLANTE
Courtesy Tulsa World

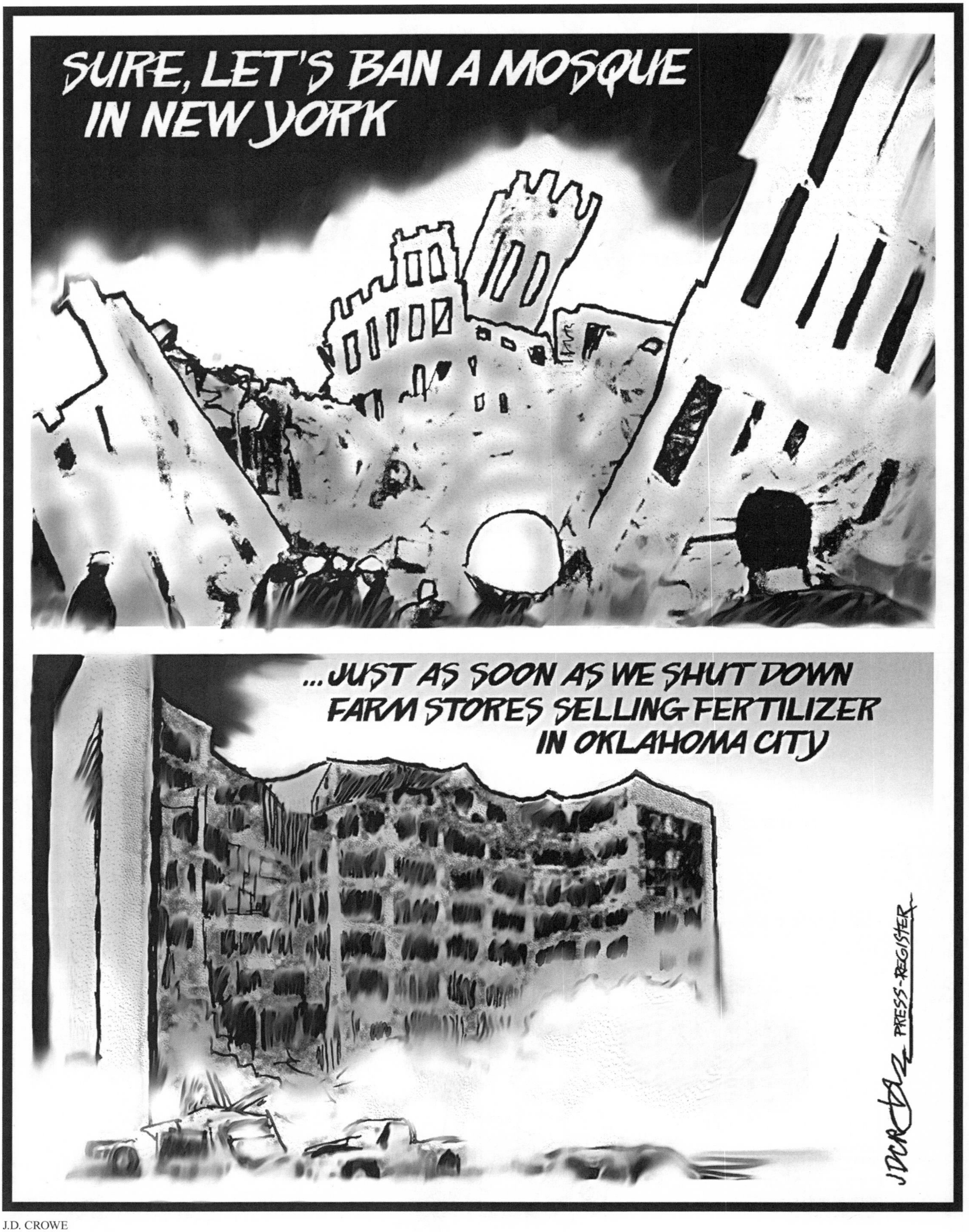
SURE, LET'S BAN A MOSQUE IN NEW YORK
...JUST AS SOON AS WE SHUT DOWN FARM STORES SELLING FERTILIZER IN OKLAHOMA CITY
PRESS-REGISTER

J.D. CROWE
Courtesy Mobile Press-Register

Ground Zero Mosque

Plans by Muslims to build a 13-story Islamic community center and mosque near the site of the 9/11 terrorist attack on the world Trade Center in New York City set off a firestorm of protest. New York Mayor Michael Bloomberg endorsed the project, but survivors of the 9/11 attack and relatives of those killed were outraged, calling the proposal a gross insult to the memory of those who were killed on that terrible day.

President Obama weighed in on the controversy, saying, "I believe that Muslims have the same right to practice their religion as everyone else in this country." For millions of Americans, however, it was not a matter of religious freedom but of sensitivity to the feelings of those who lost friends and family on 9/11. Among those who condemned the plan was former Mayor Rudy Giuliani, who called it a "desecration." He declared that "nobody would allow something like that at Pearl Harbor."

Opponents of the plan were accused of overreacting and of unfairly blaming all Muslims for the 9/11 attack. House Speaker Nancy Pelosi called for an investigation into funding of anti-mosque sentiment.

GLENN FODEN
Courtesy Artizans.com

GROUND ZERO

103

J.R ROSE
Courtesy Byrd Newspapers of Va.

JIMMY MARGULIES
Courtesy JimMarg.com

JERRY BREEN
Courtesy newbreen.com

DEB MILBRATH
Courtesy The New York Times

STEVE McBRIDE
Courtesy Independence Reporter (Kan.)

TERRY WISE
Courtesy Ratland.com

DANA SUMMERS
Courtesy Orlando Sentinel

STEPHEN RUSTAD
Courtesy Steve Rustad Blogs

JOEL PETT
Courtesy Lexington Herald-Leader

GROUND ZERO MEMORIAL

INTOLERANCE

NICK ANDERSON
Courtesy Houston Chronicle

WAYNE STROOT
Courtesy Hastings Tribune

I.P.D.:
IMPROVISED POLITICAL DEVICE

GUISE OF RELIGIOUS TOLERANCE

TICK TICK
TICK

GROUND ZERO MOSQUE

ADAM ZYGLIS
Courtesy Buffalo News

CHAN LOWE
Courtesy South Florida Sun-Sentinel/
Tribune Media Services

MILT PRIGGEE
Courtesy miltpriggee.com

NATE BEELER
Courtesy Washington Examiner

THE PROPHET PALIN

The Military

The fighting in Afghanistan continued in 2010 in America's longest war, spanning nine years. President Obama sent an additional 30,000 troops to the country as the war in Iraq was winding down.

The president fired the commander of U.S. troops in Afghanistan, Gen. Stanley McCrystal, after an article appeared in *Rolling Stone* magazine in which McCrystal was quoted as making unflattering remarks about the Obama Administration. The commander was replaced by Gen. David Petraeus, who had led the successful troop surge in Iraq. Some have speculated that Petraeus might run for president, but he denied any political ambitions.

WikiLeaks, which publishes leaks of otherwise unavailable documents, posted video that purported to show Iraqi citizens killed by U.S. forces. The international organization also released Afghan War Diary, a compilation of more than 76,900 classified U.S. military documents.

A Florida minister cancelled plans to hold a public burning of the *Quran,* Islam's holy book, after fears were expressed that it could endanger U.S. troops in Afghanistan and Iraq.

REX BABIN
Courtesy Sacramento Bee

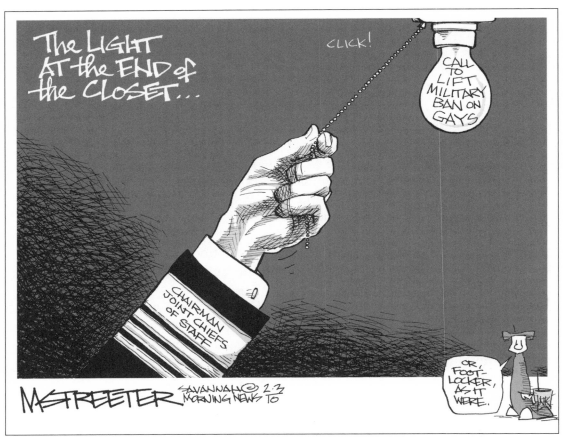

MARK STREETER
Courtesy Savannah Morning News

PAUL FELL
Courtesy Artizans Syndicate

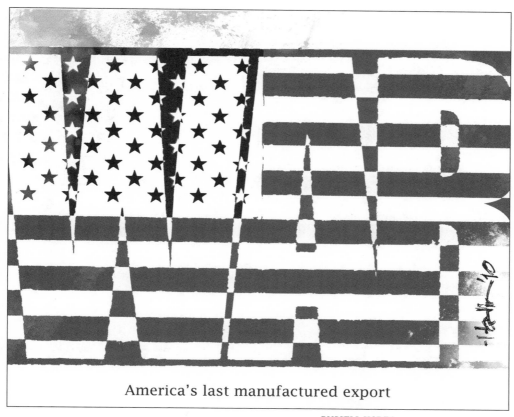

America's last manufactured export

RUSSELL HODIN
Courtesy New Times Independent Weekly (Calif.)

TIM BENSON
Courtesy Argus Leader (S.D.)

JIMMY MARGULIES
Courtesy JimMarg.com

JOSEPH O'MAHONEY
Courtesy The Patriot Ledger

MARC MURPHY
Courtesy Louisville Courier-Journal

114

MISSION ACCOMPLISHED

DENNIS DRAUGHON
Courtesy Fayetteville Observer

IRENE OLDS
Courtesy Brown County Democrat (Ind.)

ELIZABETH BRICQUET
Courtesy Kingsport Times-News

JEFF DANZIGER
Courtesy NYTS/CWS

Religious Right Wingers in Florida Burn Korans Further Infuriating Afghan Enemy

MARK STREETER
Courtesy Savannah Morning News

PHIL HANDS
Courtesy Artizans.com

JIMMY MARGULIES
Courtesy JimMarg.com

MIKE KEEFE
Courtesy Denver Post

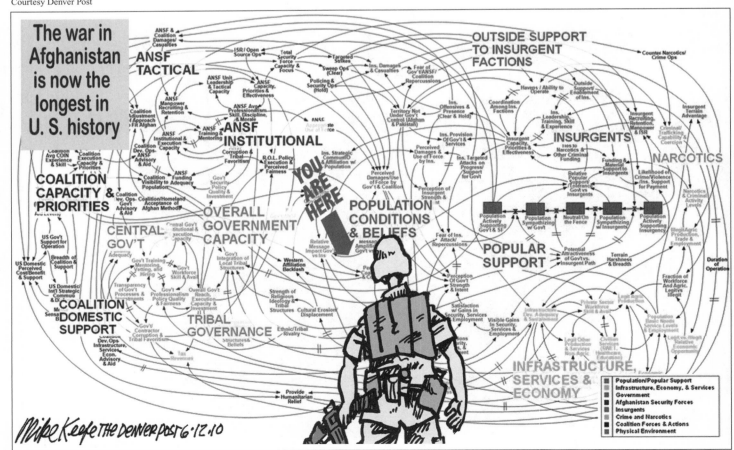

STEVE GREENBERG
Courtesy Ventura County Reporter (Calif.)

J.D. CROWE
Courtesy Mobile Press-Register

MARK BAKER
Courtesy Army Times

WILLIAM WARREN
Courtesy Liberty Features Syndicate

CHARLIE HALL
Courtesy The Rhode Island Group

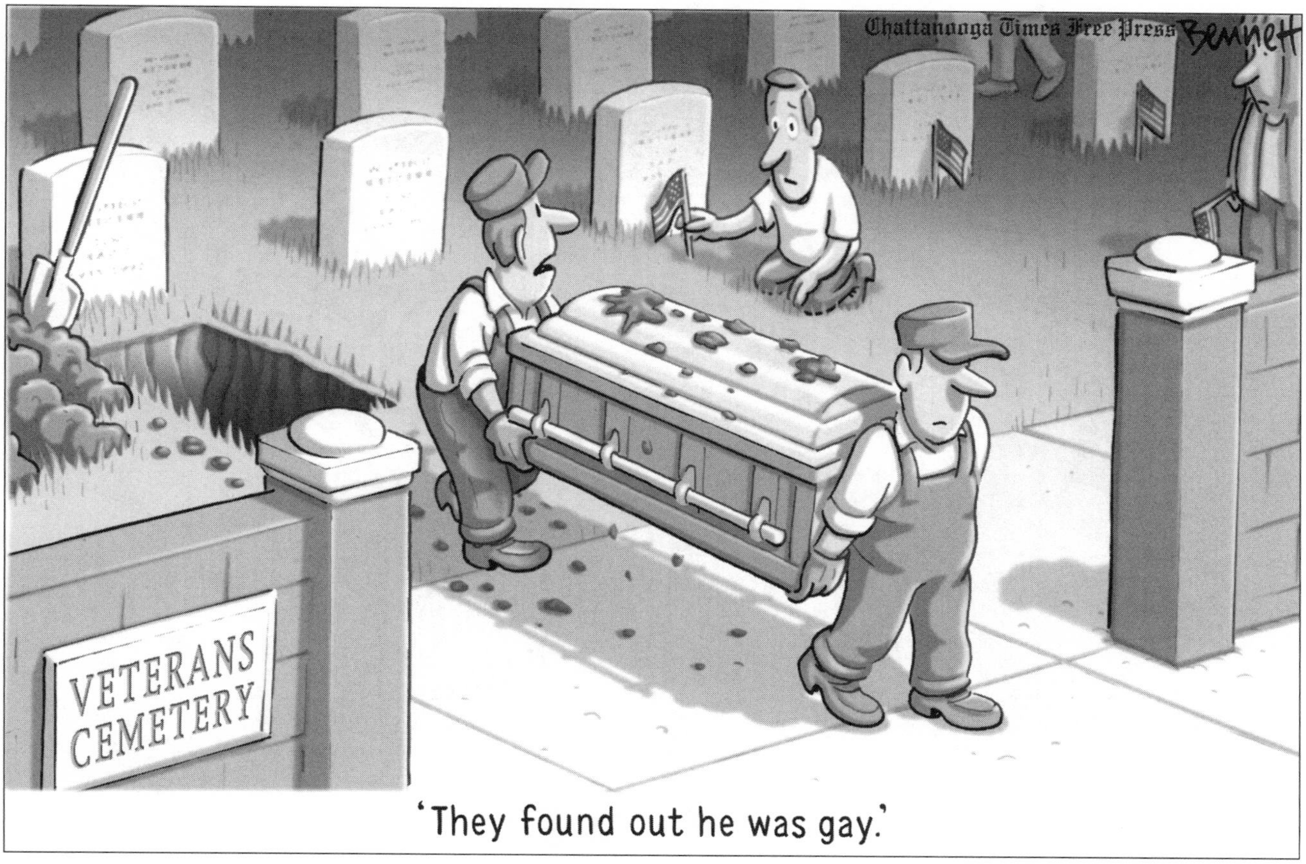
Chattanooga Times Free Press Bennett
VETERANS CEMETERY
'They found out he was gay.'

CLAY BENNETT
Courtesy Chattanooga Times-Free Press

MIKE KEEFE
Courtesy Denver Post

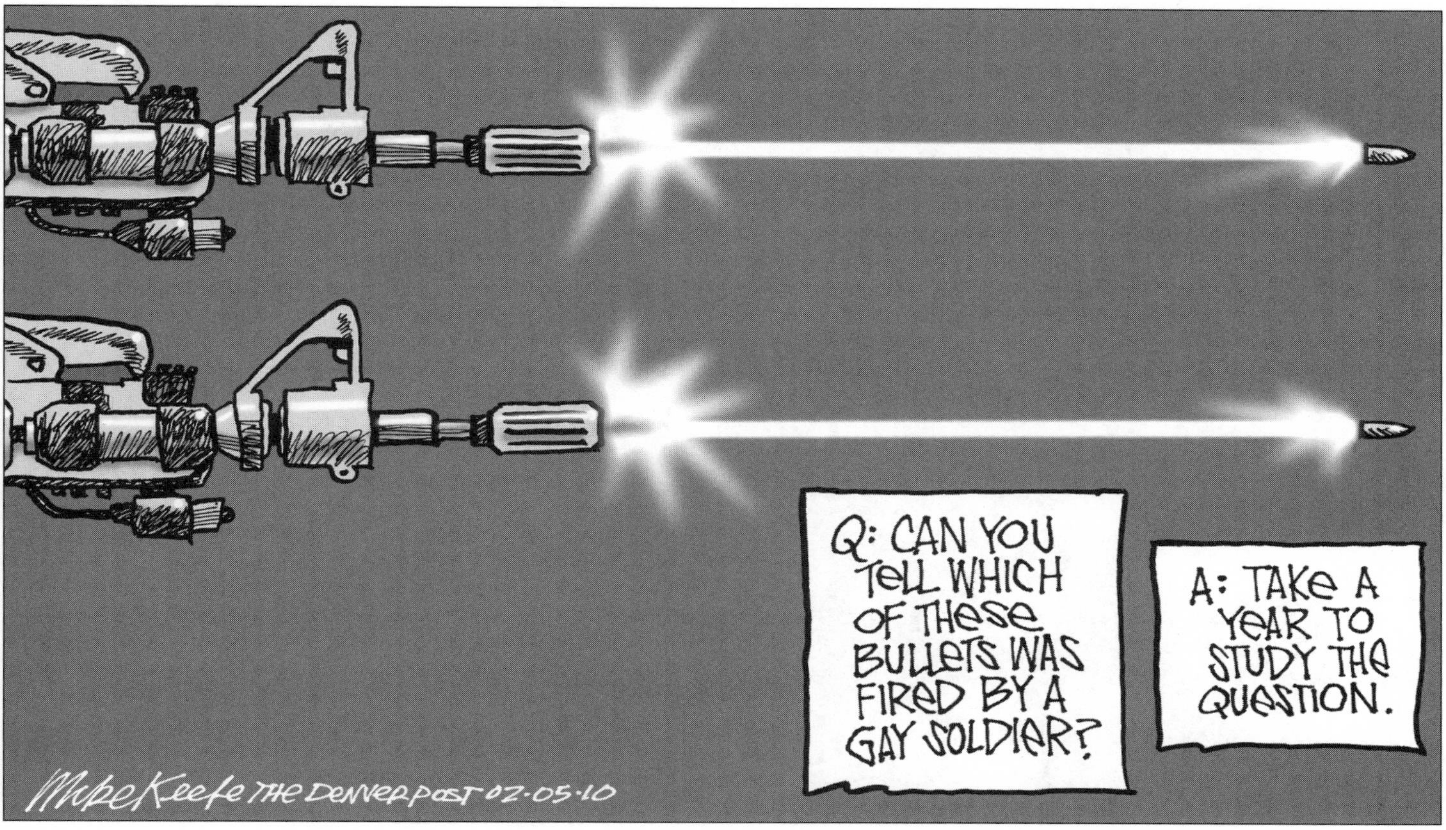
Q: CAN YOU TELL WHICH OF THESE BULLETS WAS FIRED BY A GAY SOLDIER?
A: TAKE A YEAR TO STUDY THE QUESTION.
Mike Keefe THE DENVER POST 02.05.10

JEFF DANZIGER
Courtesy NYTS/CWS

RICK KOLLINGER
Courtesy Star-Democrat (Md.)

Air Travel

American Airlines announced it was stripping the interiors of its older Boeing 737s to increase overhead luggage space, squeeze in more seats, and add new television sets. A new seat design will allow the planes to carry 160 passengers, up from 148, with a couple of inches less space between the seats.

High tech security scanners that might have prevented the would-be Christmas Day bomber from boarding a jetliner to the U.S. have been installed in only a few airports around the world. The reason? Concerns that the machines, which can "see" through clothing, invade the privacy of travelers.

After becoming frustrated by unruly passengers, a Jet Blue flight attendant shouted obscenities, grabbed a beer, and slid down the plane's emergency chute.

DANA SUMMERS
Courtesy Orlando Sentinel

DAVID BROWN
Courtesy David G. Brown Studios

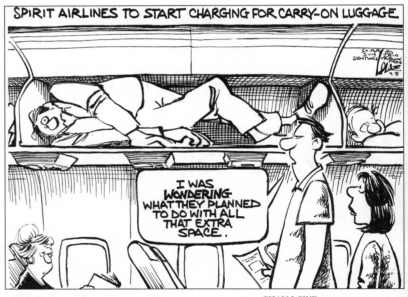

CHAN LOWE
Courtesy South Florida Sun-Sentinel/
Tribune Media Services

PAUL BERGE
Courtesy Racine Post (Wisc.)

STEVE NEASE
Courtesy Toronto Sun (Can.)

WILLIAM FLINT
Courtesy Dallas Morning News

CHARLES BEYL
Courtesy Lancaster Sunday News (Pa.)

STEPHEN RUSTAD
Courtesy Steve Rustad Blogs

Health

President Obama's healthcare reform measure remains unpopular with a majority of Americans, despite a diligent campaign to sell it to voters. According to a Rasmussen poll, 61 percent want to see it repealed outright. The poll clearly shows a large divide between mainstream voters and the political class. While 74 percent of mainstream voters favor repeal, 74 percent of the political class support the law.

Few people, including the congressmen and senators who voted for it, bothered to read the bill. House Speaker Nancy Pelosi famously declared that Congress needed to pass the bill "to find out what's in it."

Montana passed legislation making it legal for patients suffering from chronic pain, HIV, cancer, and glaucoma to use marijuana. Drug companies continue to wield major influence on Capitol Hill. An outbreak of bedbug reports led to a national bedbug summit attended by 350 experts.

Hundreds of people across the nation were sickened in a salmonella outbreak linked to eggs. California tallied 266 cases while seven other states recorded clusters of suspicious diagnoses. Health officials recalled 380 million eggs.

MILT PRIGGEE
Courtesy miltpriggee.com

SISYPHUS ACCOMPLISHED

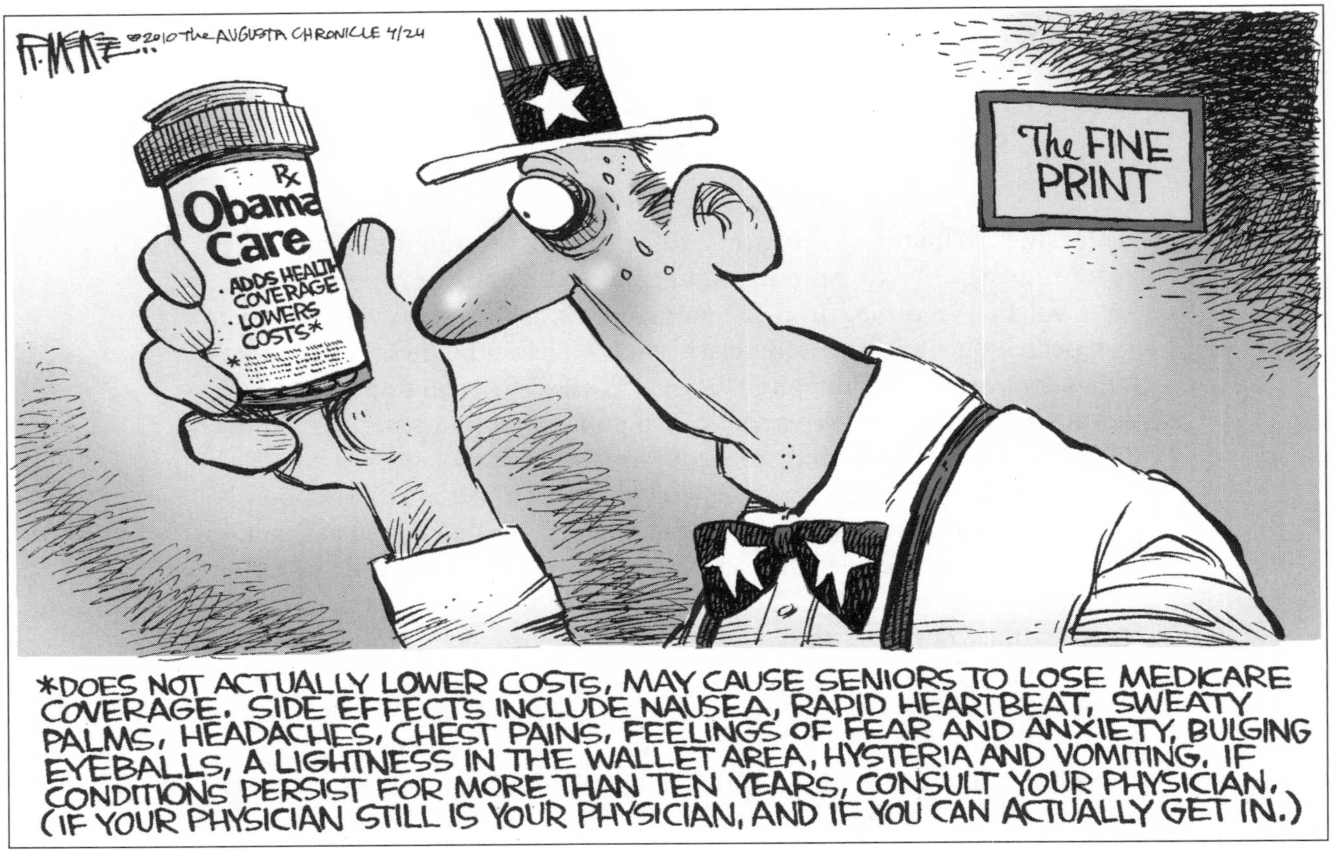
©2010 The Augusta Chronicle 4/24
Rx
Obama Care
· ADDS HEALTH COVERAGE
· LOWERS COSTS*
The FINE PRINT
*DOES NOT ACTUALLY LOWER COSTS, MAY CAUSE SENIORS TO LOSE MEDICARE COVERAGE. SIDE EFFECTS INCLUDE NAUSEA, RAPID HEARTBEAT, SWEATY PALMS, HEADACHES, CHEST PAINS, FEELINGS OF FEAR AND ANXIETY, BULGING EYEBALLS, A LIGHTNESS IN THE WALLET AREA, HYSTERIA AND VOMITING. IF CONDITIONS PERSIST FOR MORE THAN TEN YEARS, CONSULT YOUR PHYSICIAN. (IF YOUR PHYSICIAN STILL IS YOUR PHYSICIAN, AND IF YOU CAN ACTUALLY GET IN.)

RICK MCKEE
Courtesy Augusta Chronicle

CHUCK ASAY
Courtesy Creators.com

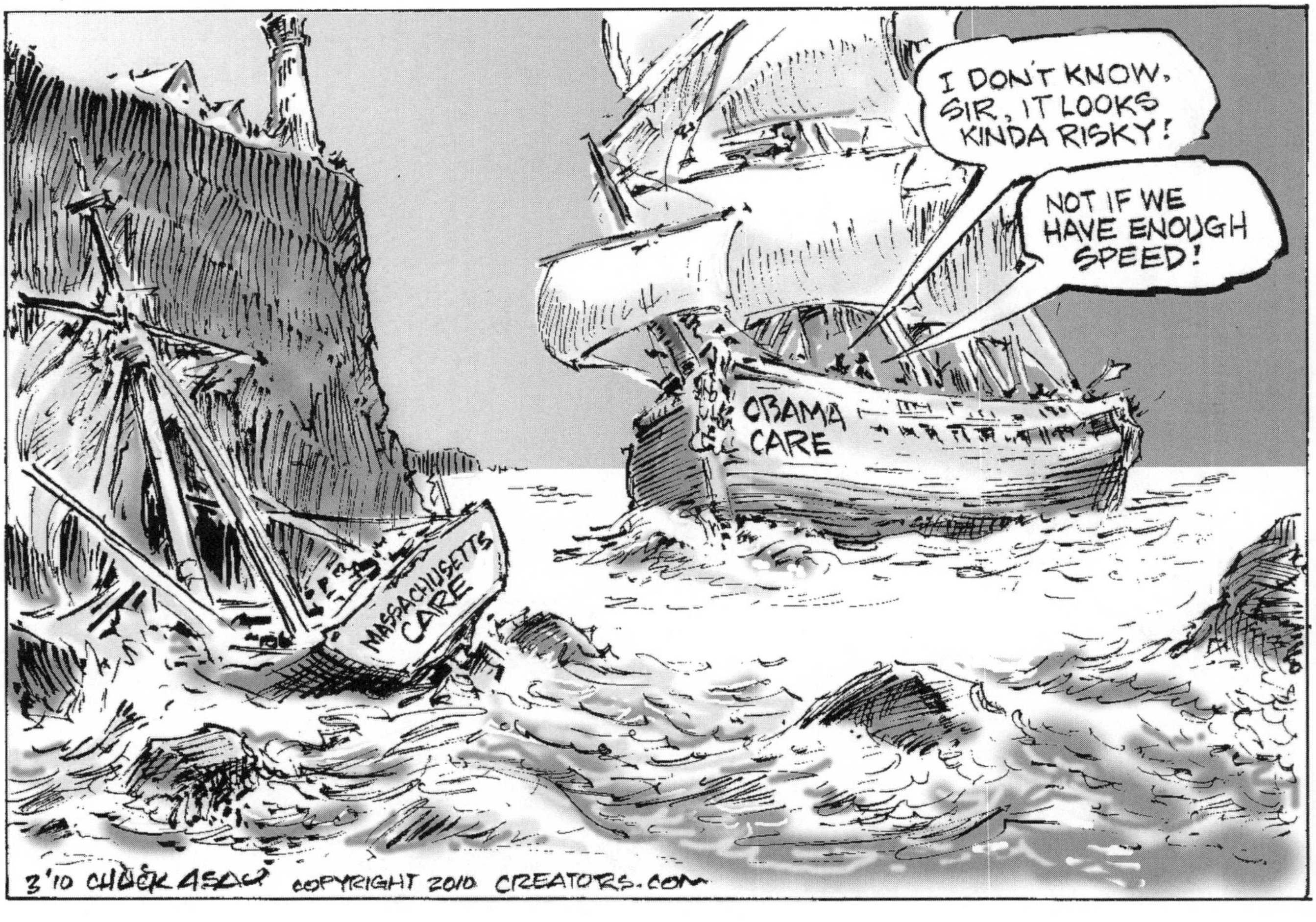
I DON'T KNOW, SIR, IT LOOKS KINDA RISKY!
NOT IF WE HAVE ENOUGH SPEED!
OBAMA CARE
MASSACHUSETTS CARE
3'10 CHUCK ASAY COPYRIGHT 2010 CREATORS.COM

JIM DYKE
Courtesy Jefferson City News-Tribune (Mo.)

JAKE FULLER
Courtesy Artizans.com

DOUGLAS REGALIA
Courtesy MRCPA.com

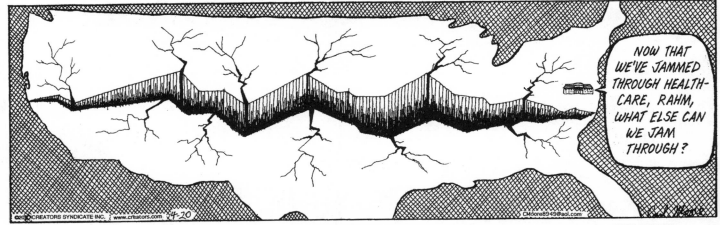

CARL MOORE
Courtesy Creators Syndicate

ROBERT ARIAIL
Courtesy ROBERTARIAIL.COM

THEO MOUDAKIS
Courtesy Toronto Star (Can.)

GARY VARVEL
Courtesy Indianapolis Star

PAUL FELL
Courtesy Artizans Syndicate

WILLIAM FLINT
Courtesy Dallas Morning News

NATIONAL HEALTH CARE REFORM.

(ALL LEFT WING)

©2009 CREATORS.COM
GORRELLART.COM
GORRELL

BOB GORRELL
Courtesy Creators.com

RANDY BISH
Courtesy Pittsburgh Tribune-Review

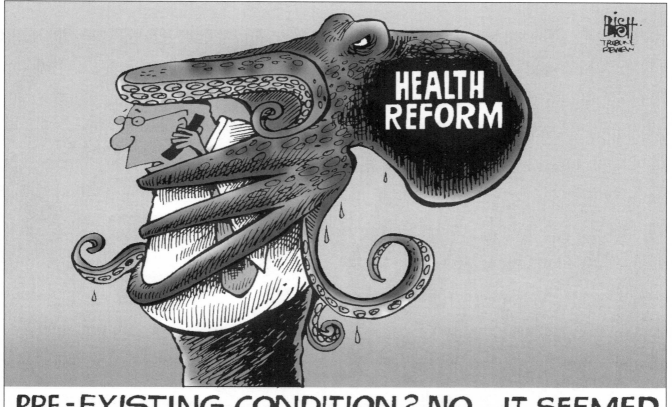

PRE-EXISTING CONDITION? NO... IT SEEMED TO JUST GRAB ON TO ME OVERNIGHT

JERRY BREEN
Courtesy newbreen.com

STEVE NEASE
Courtesy Toronto Sun (Can.)

WALT HANDELSMAN
Courtesy Newsday

VIC HARVILLE
Courtesy Stephens Media

ED HALL
Courtesy Baker County Press (Fla.)

THOMAS BECK
Courtesy Freeport Journal-Standard (Ill.)

DAVID HITCH
Courtesy Worcester Telegram & Gazette (Mass.)

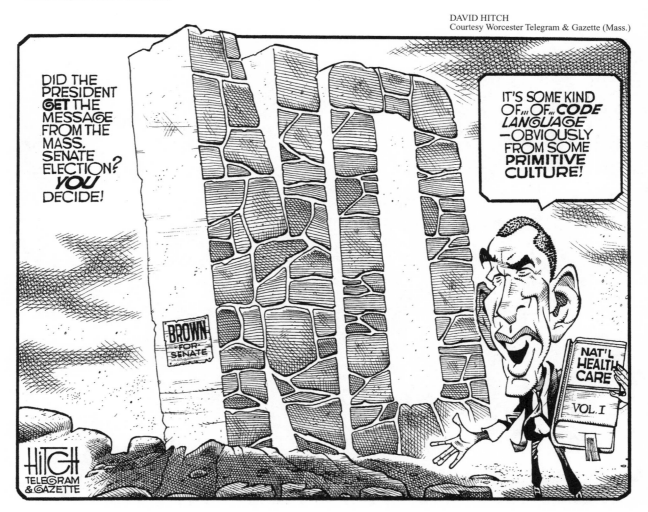

STEPHEN TEMPLETON
Courtesy Flathead Beacon.com

JOSEPH HOFFECKER
Courtesy American City Business Journals

ADAM ZYGLIS
Courtesy Buffalo News

DAVID HORSEY
Courtesy Hearst Newspapers

The Courts

In response to Chicago's strong gun-control law, the U.S. Supreme Court ruled that Americans in all fifty states have a constitutional right to possess firearms for self-defense. The legal battle over the right to possess firearms heated up in earnest two years ago in a court challenge to a strict Washington, D.C. law.

The court struck down a major portion of a 2002 campaign finance-reform law, saying it violates the free-speech rights of corporations to engage in public debate. The ruling means corporations can spend freely on political ads. President Obama, in his State of the Union address, berated the court for its ruling.

Obama nominated Elena Kagan to become the fourth female justice on the U.S. Supreme Court. She was confirmed handily by the Senate and sworn in August 7 by Chief Justice Roberts. She is expected to be a solid liberal vote on the court.

JAMES MCCLOSKEY
Courtesy Staunton News-Leader (Va.)

TIM HARTMAN
Courtesy Beaver County Times (Pa.

SCOTT STANTIS
Courtesy Chicago Tribune

ROSS R. GOSSE
Courtesy EDITOONS, iNCK.

HAP PITKIN
Courtesy Boulder Camera

Education

Violence continued to pose problems for schools during the year. A CBS News poll found that although 96 percent of students felt safe while attending class, 22 percent of the same students said they knew classmates who regularly carried weapons to school. More than half believed that a shooting could take place at their school.

The Texas Board of Education approved a number of controversial and conservatively slanted revisions in the state's textbooks. Among them: Sen. Joseph R. McCarthy was justified in the anti-communist blacklisting actions he took during the early 1950s. The approved texts also conclude that after the collapse of the Soviet Union, documents were found confirming there were Russian spies in the U.S., that the Founding Fathers may not have intended that there be separation of church and state, and that the theory of evolution and the concept of creationism are counterbalanced issues.

The changes may have ramifications nationwide since Texas buys so many textbooks that publishers may sometimes provide the same books to other states at discounted rates.

STEVEN LAIT
Courtesy Oakland Tribune

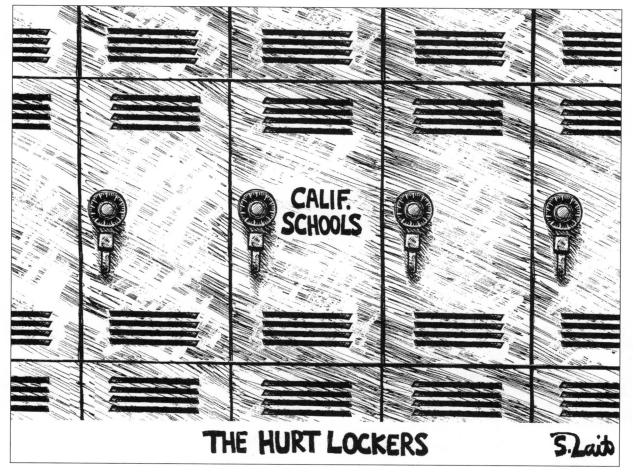

143

STEVEN PARRA
Courtesy Fresno Bee

"NO, YOU STILL HAVE TO WRITE A REPORT ABOUT WHAT YOU DID ON YOUR SUMMER VACATION...I HAVEN'T BEEN FOLLOWING YOUR TWEETS..."

DANIEL FENECH
Courtesy Heritage Newspapers/
Journal-Register Co.

CHARLIE HALL
Courtesy The Rhode Island Group

144

STEVEN LAIT
Courtesy Oakland Tribune

IRENE OLDS
Courtesy Brown County Democrat (Ind.)

JESSE SPRINGER
Courtesy Eugene Register-Guard

DENNIS DRAUGHON
Courtesy Fayetteville Observer

Sports

Professional golfer Tiger Woods, the world's richest athlete, acknowledged that he had been unfaithful to his wife and was undergoing therapy. Woods returned to golf competition after a 20-week break but his post-affair game was not up to par. He previously had dominated the sport.

Professional basketball player LeBron James made big news when he became a free agent and found a number of teams bidding for his services. He eventually signed a long-term contract with the Miami Heat that was rumored to be in the $100-million range.

Former major league pitcher Roger Clemens was indicted by a federal grand jury on charges of making false statements to Congress about the use of performance-enhancing drugs. Baseball managers Bobby Cox, Joe Torre, and Lou Piniella announced their retirements.

The 2010 Winter Olympics were held in Vancouver, and Brett Favre, who has made a career out of retiring, signed with the Minnesota Vikings. College athletics seemed to be near a major realignment of conferences.

STEVE KELLEY
Courtesy Times-Picayune (La.)

PAUL FELL
Courtesy Artizans Syndicate

RANDY BISH
Courtesy Pittsburgh Tribune-Review

VIC HARVILLE
Courtesy Stephens Media

148

STEVEN LAIT
Courtesy Oakland Tribune

JOSEPH O'MAHONEY
Courtesy The Patriot Ledger

CHRIS BRITT
Courtesy State Journal-Register (Ill.)

WILLIAM FLINT
Courtesy Dallas Morning News

WILLIAM O'TOOLE
Courtesy OppositePicks.net

MIKE SPICER
Courtesy Mike Spicer

151

TONY BAYER
Courtesy Tonybayertoons.com

RICK MCKEE
Courtesy Augusta Chronicle

TIM BENSON
Courtesy Argus Leader (S.D.

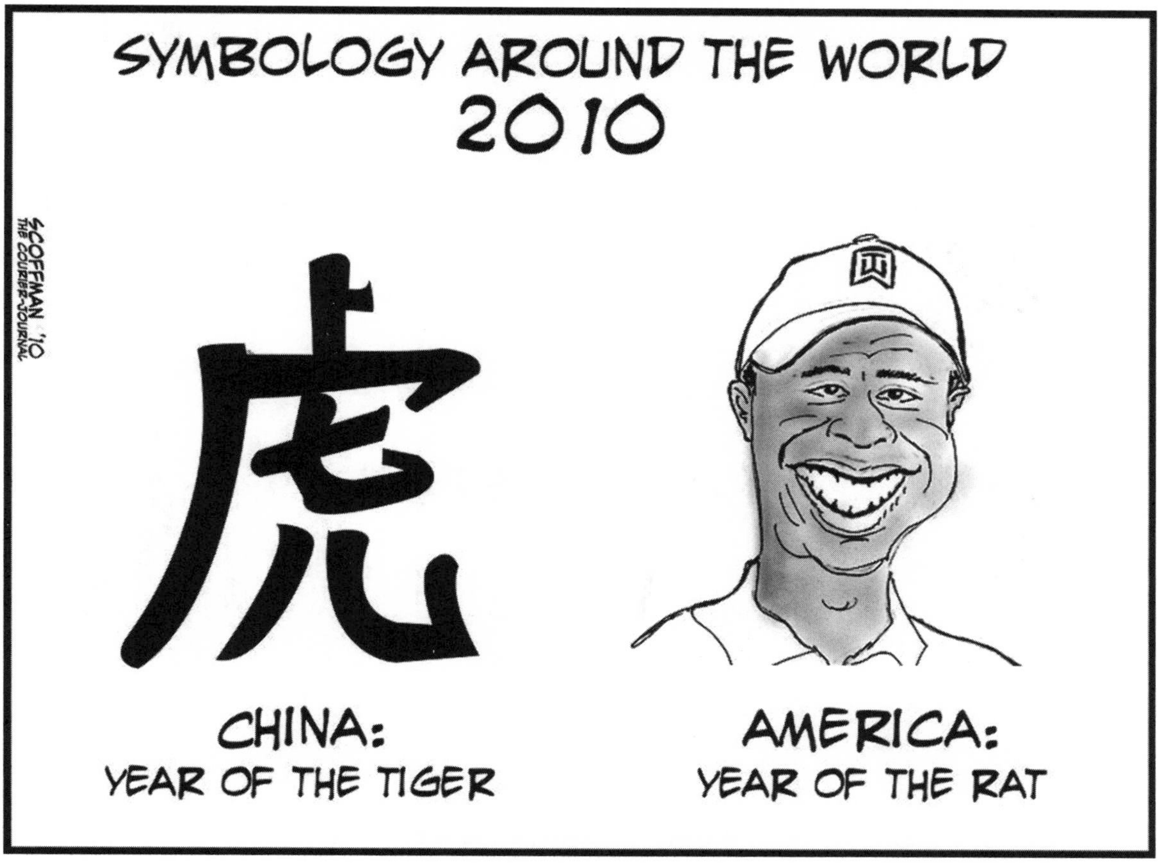
SYMBOLOGY AROUND THE WORLD
2010
虎
CHINA:
YEAR OF THE TIGER
AMERICA:
YEAR OF THE RAT

SCOTT COFFMAN
Courtesy Louisville Courier-Journal

TERRY WISE
Courtesy Ratland.com

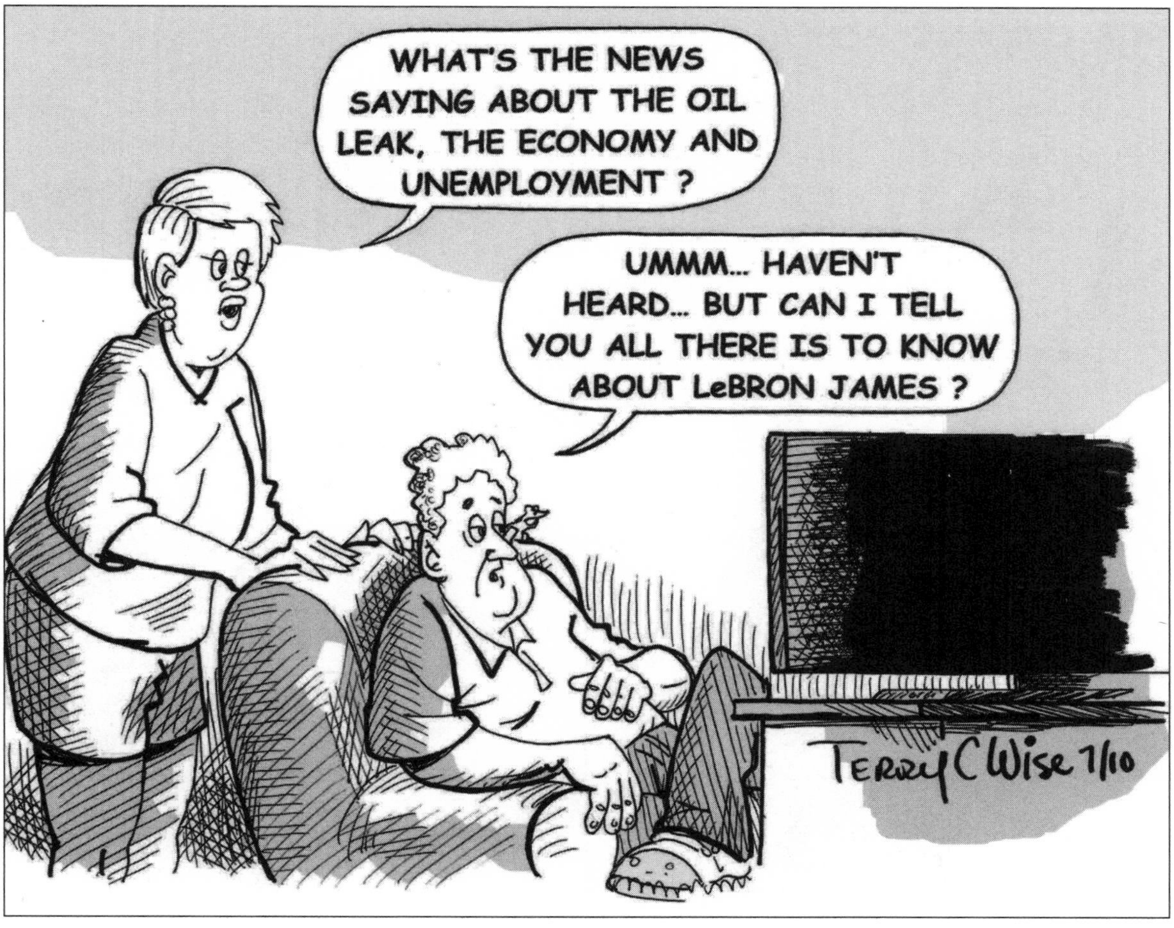
WHAT'S THE NEWS SAYING ABOUT THE OIL LEAK, THE ECONOMY AND UNEMPLOYMENT ?
UMMM... HAVEN'T HEARD... BUT CAN I TELL YOU ALL THERE IS TO KNOW ABOUT LeBRON JAMES ?
TERRY C WISE 7/10

POPULISM IN THE U.S. IN 2010.

PITKIN '10
BOULDER CAMERA

LAST WEEKEND, SOME 200,000 TEA PARTY PARTICIPANTS GATHERED...

TO BE INSPIRED BY GLENN BECK, A "POPULIST" WHO MAKES ABOUT $32 MILLION A YEAR.

AND WHOSE KEY SUPPORTERS INCLUDE BILLIONAIRES RUPERT MURDOCH AND CHARLES AND DAVID KOCH.

HAP PITKIN
Courtesy Boulder Camera

JOHN SHERFFIUS
Courtesy Boulder Camera

SHERFFIUS
Boulder Camera © 8/27/10 creators.com
jsherffius@gmail.com
sherffius.com

King

Clown

Society

Popular Libertarian radio and television talk show host Glenn Beck held a "Restoring Honor" rally in Washington, D.C. on August 28, the anniversary of Martin Luther King's historic "I Have A Dream" speech. A crowd estimated at 300,000 filled the mall from the Lincoln Memorial to the Washington Memorial. The event was billed as a spiritual awakening and a non-political salute to the military.

Many environmentalists, although opposed to offshore drilling, continued to drive their gas guzzlers and jet around the country in private aircraft. BP executives and officials of many other oil companies continued to blame each other for the nation's worst oil spill ever.

2010 Census figures showed that the income gap between the richest and the poorest Americans grew to the widest on record. Supporters of gay marriage rights rallied for their cause in Manhattan, and Conan O'Brien quit "The Tonight Show" after a programming dispute.

A Florida minister caused an up-roar when he threatened to burn copies of the *Quran,* Islam's holy book. After almost universal condemnation, he gave up the idea.

ROBERT UNELL
Courtesy Kansas City Star

NATIONAL DEBATE ON
BIRTH CONTROL, SEX EDUCATION,
AND POPULATION

JOEL PETT
Courtesy Lexington Herald-Leader

GENE HERNDON
Courtesy Kokomo Tribune

PAUL BERGE
Courtesy Racine Post (Wisc.)

MIKE LUCKOVICH
Courtesy Atlanta Journal-Constitution

MICHAEL RAMIREZ
Courtesy Investor's Business Daily

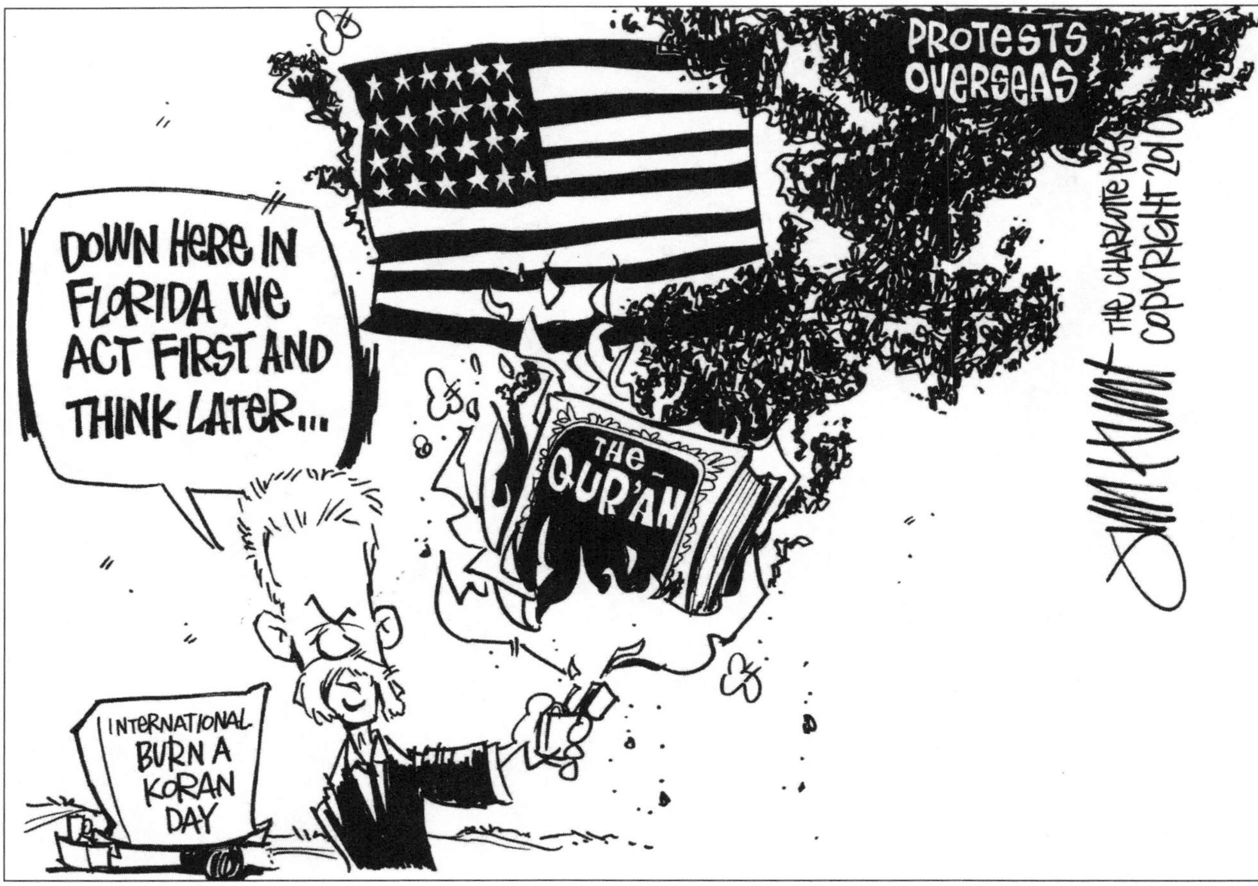
PROTESTS OVERSEAS
DOWN HERE IN FLORIDA WE ACT FIRST AND THINK LATER...
THE QUR'AN
INTERNATIONAL BURN A KORAN DAY
THE CHARLOTTE POST COPYRIGHT 2010
JIM HUNT

JIM HUNT
Courtesy Charlotte Post

TOM STIGLICH
Courtesy TOMSTIGLICH.COM

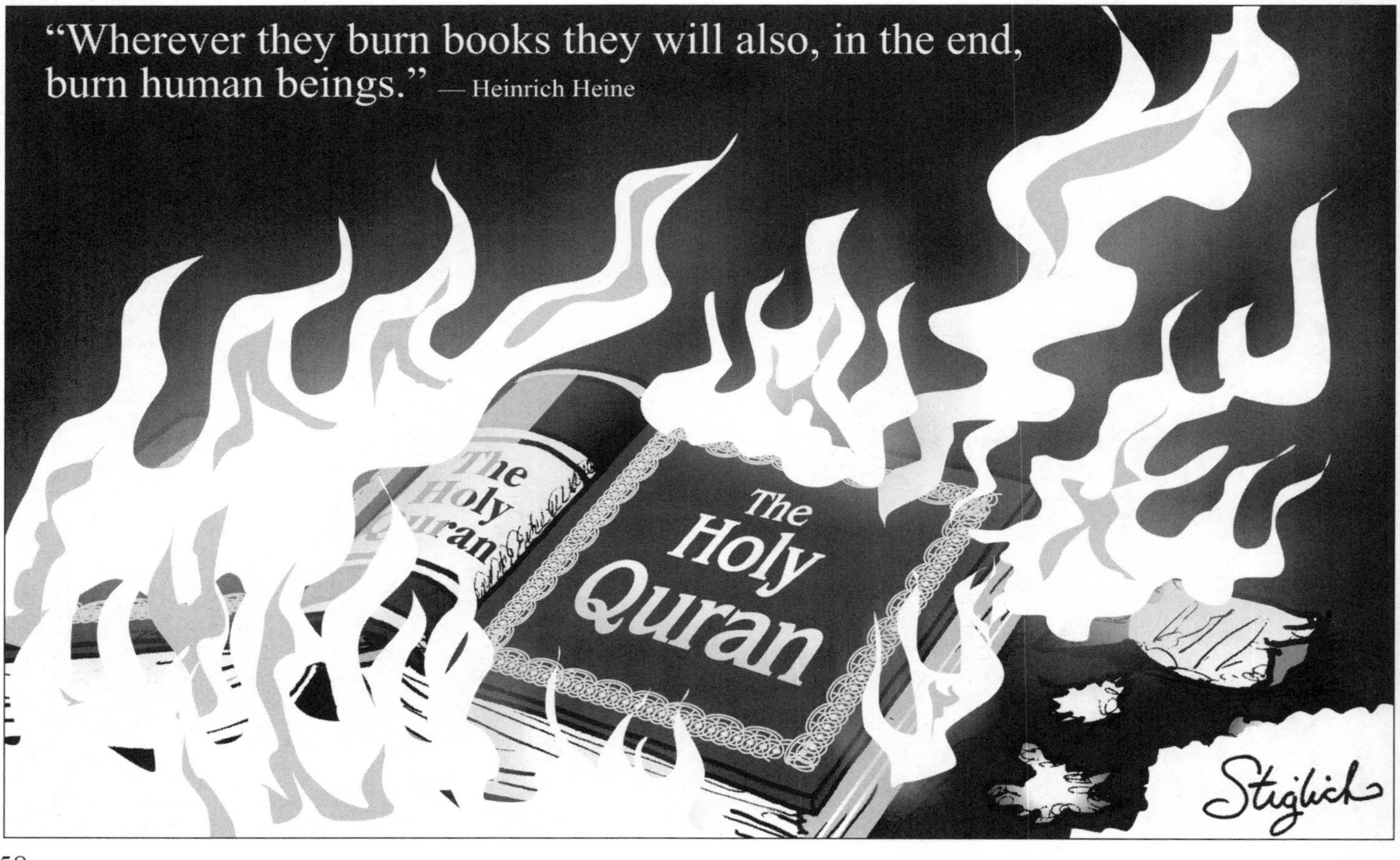
"Wherever they burn books they will also, in the end, burn human beings." — Heinrich Heine
The Holy Quran
The Holy Quran
Stiglich

FRED MULHEARN
Courtesy The Advocate (La.)

DOUGLAS REGALIA
Courtesy MRCPA.com

DANIEL FENECH
Courtesy Heritage Newspapers/
    Journal-Register Co.

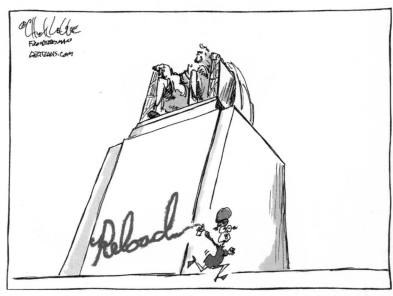

CHUCK LEGGE
Courtesy The Frontiersman

LISA BENSON
Courtesy Washington Post Writers Group

JOE KING
Courtesy Joe King

CHARLIE DANIEL
Courtesy Knoxville News-Sentinel

JOSEPH O'MAHONEY
Courtesy The Patriot Ledger

JEFF DARCY
Courtesy The Plain Dealer (Oh.)

JEFF STAHLER
Courtesy Columbus Dispatch

162

GARY VARVEL
Courtesy Indianapolis Star

JIM BUSH
Courtesy Providence Journal

DON LANDGREN, JR.
Courtesy Don Landgren, Jr.

JOSEPH HOFFECKER
Courtesy American City Business Journals

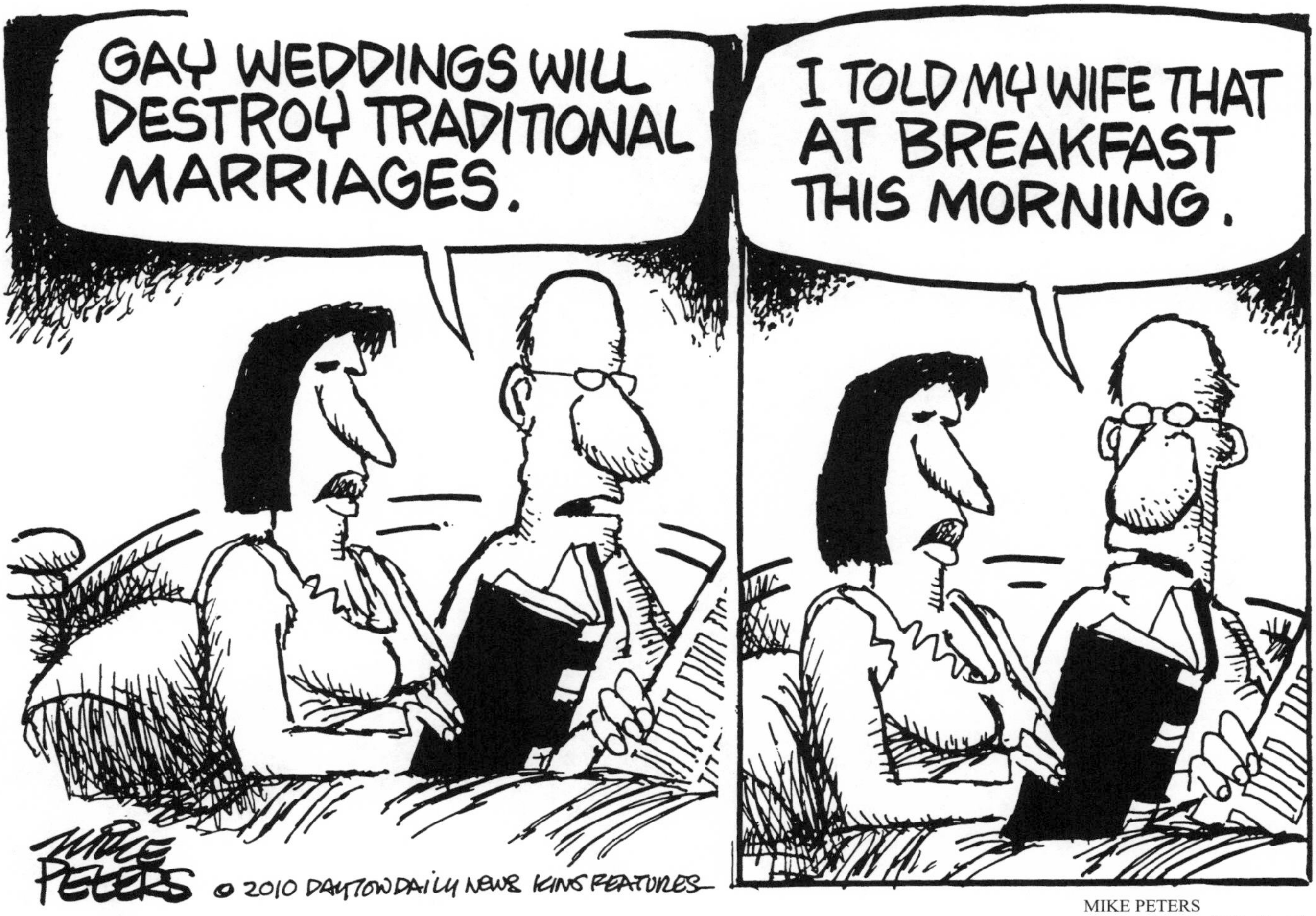
GAY WEDDINGS WILL DESTROY TRADITIONAL MARRIAGES.
I TOLD MY WIFE THAT AT BREAKFAST THIS MORNING.
MIKE PETERS
© 2010 DAYTON DAILY NEWS KING FEATURES

MIKE PETERS
Courtesy Dayton Daily News/ King Features

LYNN CARLSON/ BILL SMITH
Courtesy Lompoc Record

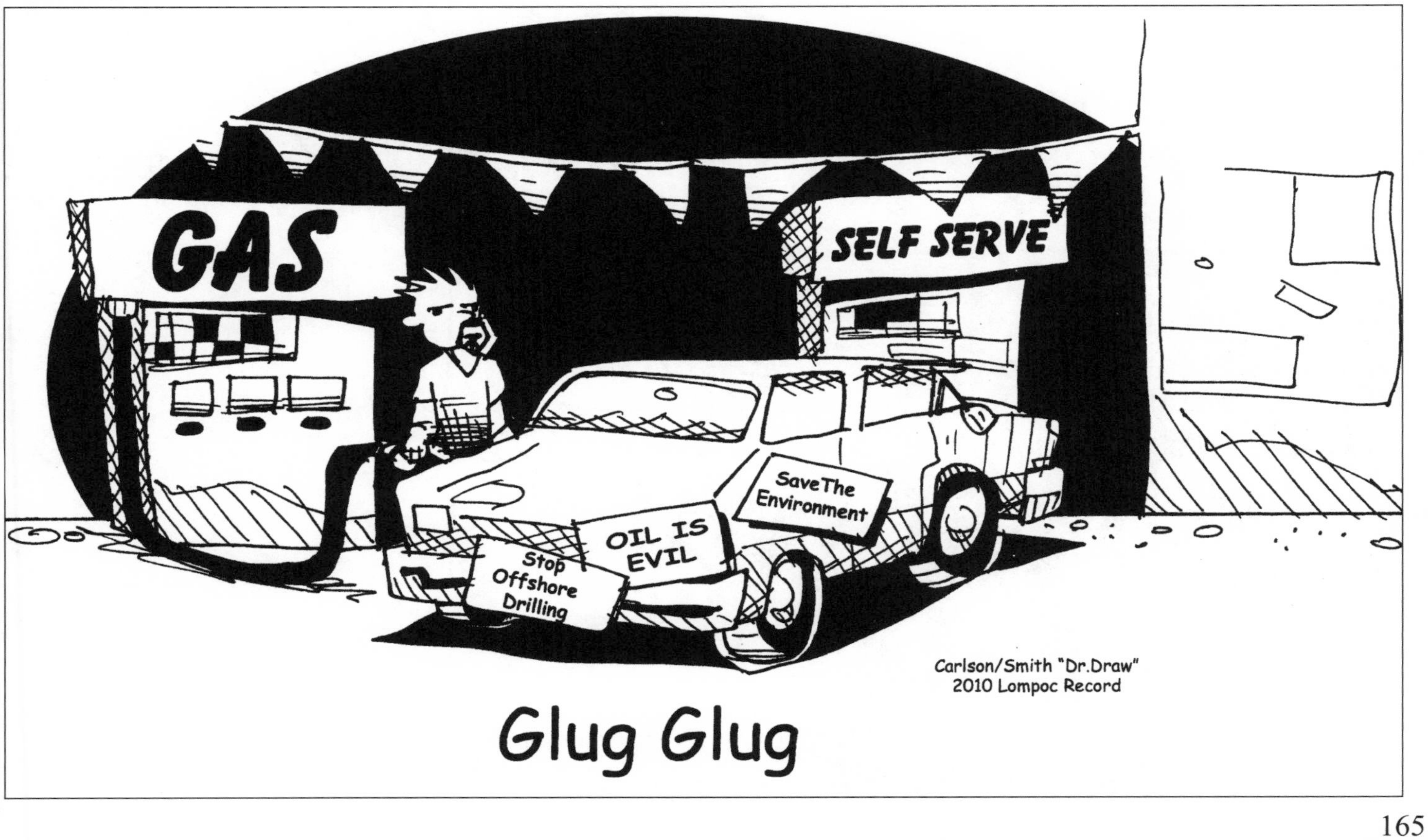
GAS
SELF SERVE
Save The Environment
OIL IS EVIL
Stop Offshore Drilling
Carlson/Smith "Dr.Draw"
2010 Lompoc Record
Glug Glug

LYNN CARLSON/ BILL SMITH
Courtesy Lompoc Record

RICHARD BARTHOLOMEW
Courtesy Artizans.com

ROGER SCHILLERSTROM
Courtesy Crain Communications

ED GAMBLE
Courtesy Florida Times-Union

MICHAEL RAMIREZ
Courtesy Investor's Business Daily

JERRY GARDEN
Courtesy Garden ARToons

DARREL AKERS
Courtesy Vacaville Reporter (Calif.)

ELIZABETH BRICQUET
Courtesy Kingsport Times-News

DON LANDGREN, JR.
Courtesy Don Landgren, Jr.

MARTY RISKIN
Courtesy Penspeak

DANIEL FITZGERALD
Courtesy Louisville Courier-Journal

MIKE LUCKOVICH
Courtesy Atlanta Journal-Constitution

The Environment

In April, drilling giant BP's Deepwater Horizon oil rig in the Gulf of Mexico exploded and sank, killing 11 workers. The damaged well eventually spewed into the ocean more than 4 million barrels of crude oil, enough to fill two supertankers. Oil invaded Louisiana's sensitive Mississippi River Delta and washed ashore in Mississippi, Alabama, and Florida.

Both the Obama Administration and BP came under heavy criticism for failing to act quickly to contain the spill. Obama ordered a moratorium on deepwater drilling, a move *The Wall Street Journal* contended could result in the loss of 75,000 jobs. The moratorium was later rescinded.

The eruption of a volcano in Iceland caused chaos in travel and lost revenue for airlines in April and May after vast swatches of European airspace were closed. Hurricane Earl followed a path up the eastern seaboard, causing significant damage.

An earthquake in Haiti left 230,000 dead and a million homeless. Broadcaster Pat Robertson said Haiti had been "cursed" because of "a pact with the devil."

MARC MURPHY
Courtesy Louisville Courier-Journal

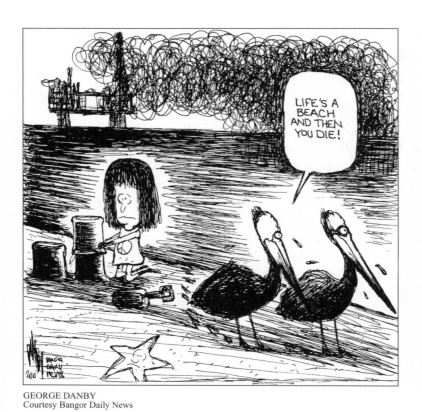

GEORGE DANBY
Courtesy Bangor Daily News

J.D. CROWE
Courtesy Mobile Press-Register

MARK STREETER
Courtesy Savannah Morning News

JOE HELLER
Courtesy Green Bay Press

BOB GORRELL
Courtesy Creators.com

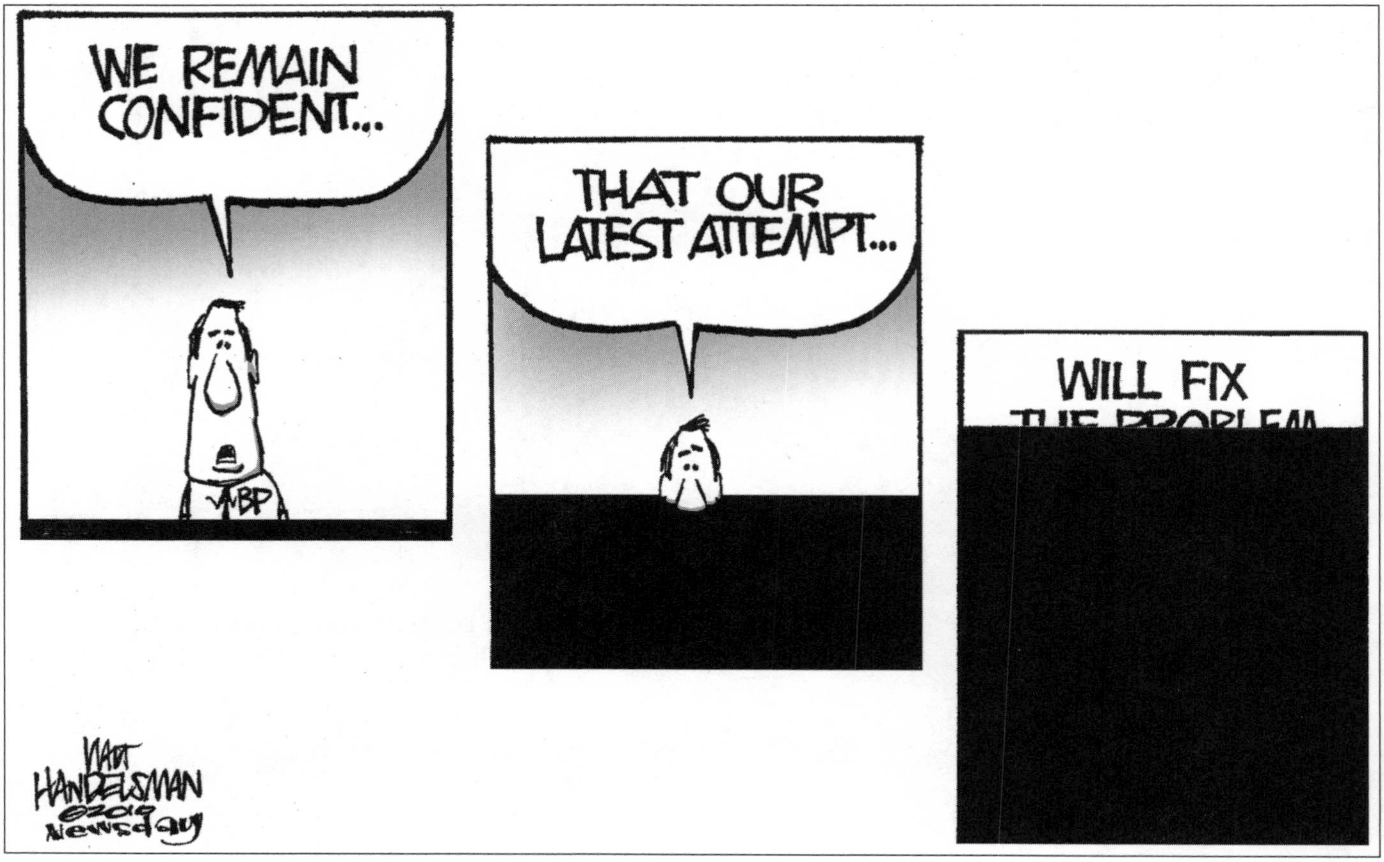
WE REMAIN CONFIDENT...
BP
THAT OUR LATEST ATTEMPT...
WILL FIX
WALT HANDELSMAN ©2010 Newsday

WALT HANDELSMAN
Courtesy Newsday

RICK MCKEE
Courtesy Augusta Chronicle

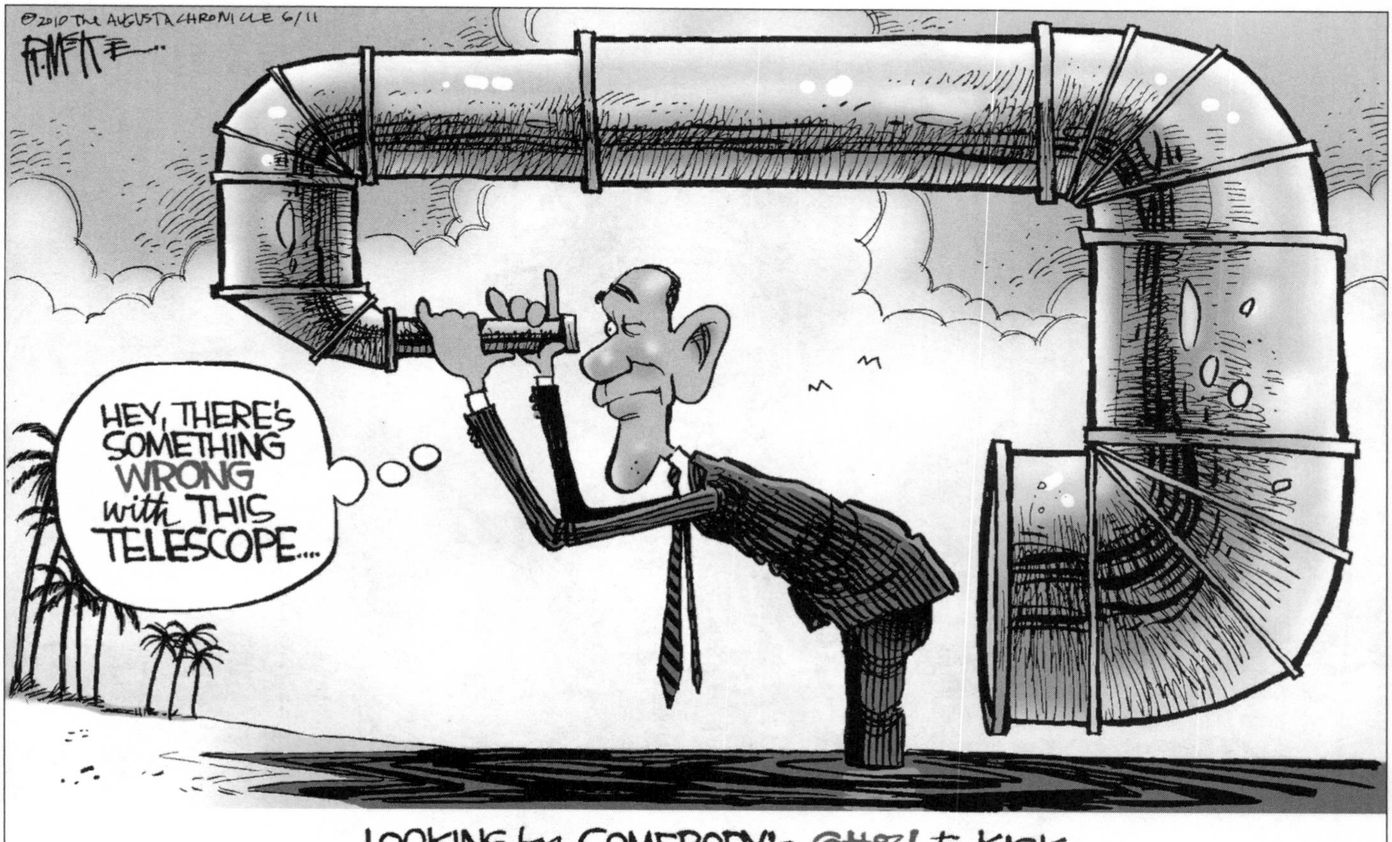
©2010 The Augusta Chronicle 6/11
R. McKEE
HEY, THERE'S SOMETHING WRONG with THIS TELESCOPE....

LOOKING for SOMEBODY's @#%! to KICK

JEFF DARCY
Courtesy The Plain Dealer (Oh.)

STEVE KELLEY
Courtesy Times-Picayune (La.)

GUY BADEAUX
Courtesy Le Droit (Can.)

FRED CURATOLO
Courtesy See Magazine

GEOFFREY MOSS
Courtesy Creators Syndicate

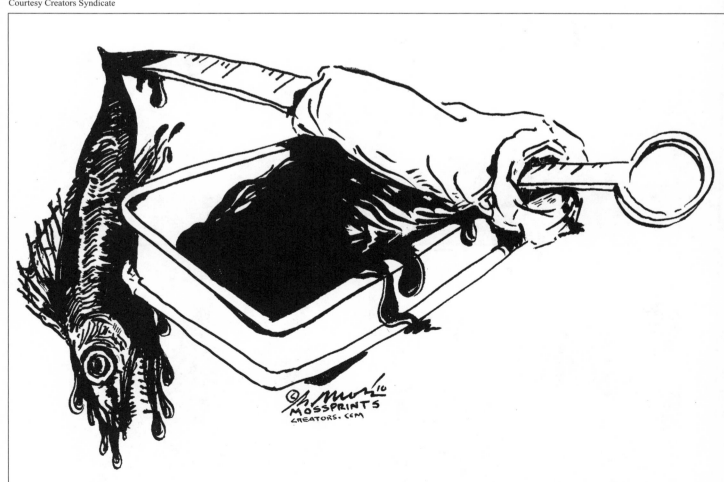

176

CHAN LOWE
Courtesy South Florida Sun-Sentinel/
Tribune Media Services

RICHARD BARTHOLOMEW
Courtesy Artizans.com

J.D. CROWE
Courtesy Mobile Press-Register

ROGER SCHILLERSTROM
Courtesy Crain Communications

MARC MURPHY
Courtesy Louisville Courier-Journal

178

Chattanooga Times Free Press Bennett
CLAY BENNETT
Courtesy Chattanooga Times-Free Press

ED GAMBLE
Courtesy Florida Times-Union

STEVE NEASE
Courtesy Toronto Sun (Can.)

TIM DOLIGHAN
Courtesy Toronto Sun (Can.)

DAVID DONAR
Courtesy McComb Daily (Miss.)

CHARLIE HALL
Courtesy The Rhode Island Group

STEVE LINDSTROM
Courtesy Duluth News-Tribune

STEVE EDWARDS
Courtesy edwardscartoons

JUSTIN DEFREITAS
Courtesy Berkeley Daily Planet

TONY BAYER
Courtesy Tonybayertoons.com

VIC HARVILLE
Courtesy Stephens Media

GENE HERNDON
Courtesy Kokomo Tribune

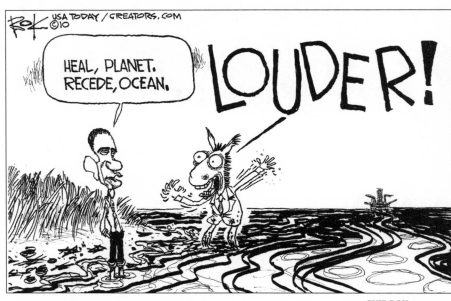

CHIP BOK
Courtesy Creators.com

ROBERT ARIAIL
Courtesy ROBERTARIAIL.COM

STEVE BREEN
Courtesy San Diego Union-Tribune

REX BABIN
Courtesy Sacramento Bee

HAP PITKIN
Courtesy Boulder Camera

JOHN TREVER
Courtesy Albuquerque Journal

THOMAS BECK
Courtesy Freeport Journal-Standard (Ill.)

MIKE BECKOM
Courtesy Index-Journal (S.C.)

JAMES MCCLOSKEY
Courtesy Staunton News-Leader (Va.)

DAVID HORSEY
Courtesy Hearst Newspapers

... and Other Issues

An Arizona law aimed at curbing illegal immigration ignited a clamorous controversy. Opponents claimed the law would lead to racial profiling. The government jumped into the fray, filing suit against Arizona on the grounds the state was usurping federal authority.

An inspector general report documented problems at Arlington National Cemetery. Officials had placed the wrong headstones on tombs, buried coffins in too-shallow graves, and interred bodies on top of one another.

An explosion at a West Virginia coal mine killed 29 miners. Toyota recalled 10 million vehicles worldwide because of safety issues. In a pastoral letter to Irish Catholics, Pope Benedict XVI condemned child abuse by priests. Chelsea Clinton was married in an elaborate affair, and Apple launched its new personal computer, the iPad.

National Public Radio news analyst Juan Williams was fired in October for expressing his concerns about Muslims.

Notables who died during the year included former secretary of state Alexander Haig and celebrated editorial cartoonist Paul Conrad.

ROBERT ARIAIL
Courtesy Spartanburg Herald-Journal

MIKE BECKOM
Courtesy Index-Journal (S.C.)

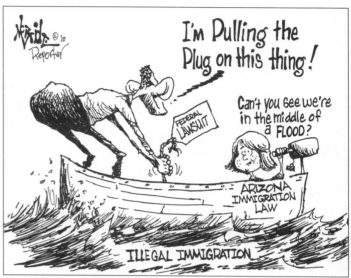

STEVE MCBRIDE
Courtesy Independence Reporter (Kan.)

JOHN SHERFFIUS
Courtesy Boulder Camera

JON RICHARDS
Courtesy jonrichardsplace.com

STEVE ARTLEY
Courtesy artleytoons.com

REX BABIN
Courtesy Sacramento Bee

STEVE LINDSTROM
Courtesy Duluth News-Tribune

JEFF DARCY
Courtesy The Plain Dealer (Oh.)

MIKE PETERS
Courtesy Dayton Daily News/
King Features

In Arizona, Governor Brewer is No Longer a Head... er... ahead... oh, never mind

JEFF DANZIGER
Courtesy NYTS/CWS

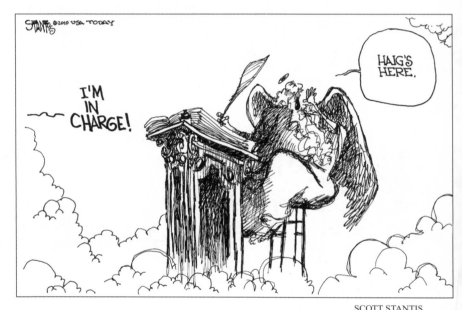

SCOTT STANTIS
Courtesy Chicago Tribune

ROSS R. GOSSE
Courtesy EDITOONS,iNCK

BOB ENGLEHART
Courtesy Hartford Courant

MIKE LUCKOVICH
Courtesy Atlanta Journal-Constitution

WILLIAM FLINT
Courtesy Dallas Morning News

ED GAMBLE
Courtesy Florida Times-Union

196

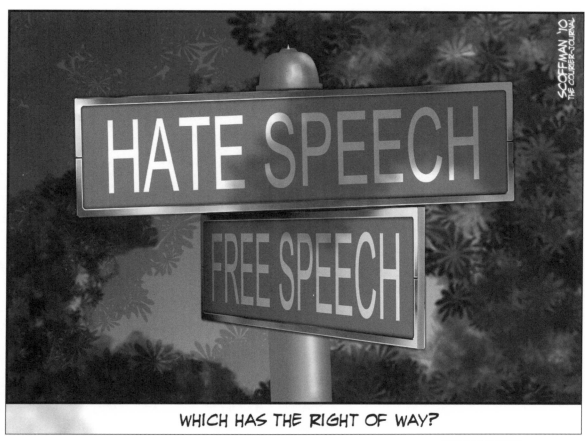

WHICH HAS THE RIGHT OF WAY?

SCOTT COFFMAN
Courtesy Louisville Courier-Journal

GARY VARVEL
Courtesy Indianapolis Star

ROBERT ARIAIL
Courtesy ROBERTARIAIL.COM

TAYLOR JONES
Courtesy Cagle Cartoons

LISA BENSON
Courtesy Washington Post Writers Group

198

WILLIAM WARREN
Courtesy Liberty Features Syndicate

BILL GARNER
Courtesy Creators.com

CLAY BENNETT
Courtesy Chattanooga Times-Free Press

KIRK ANDERSON
Courtesy KIRKtoons.com

DAN CARINO
Courtesy Capitol Weekly (Calif.)

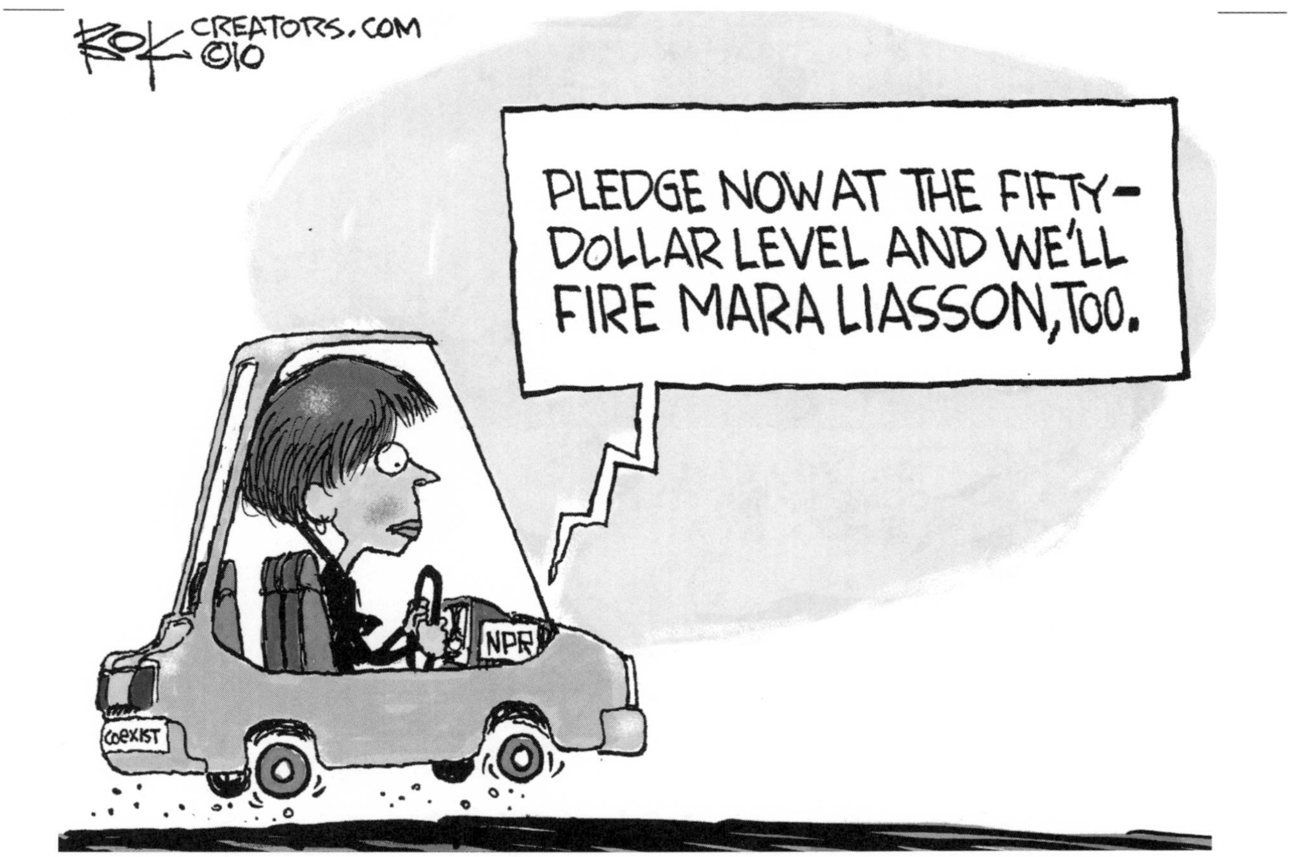
BOK CREATORS.COM ©10
PLEDGE NOW AT THE FIFTY-DOLLAR LEVEL AND WE'LL FIRE MARA LIASSON, TOO.
NPR
COEXIST

CHIP BOK
Courtesy Creators.com

MIKE SCOTT
Courtesy New Jersey Newsroom.com

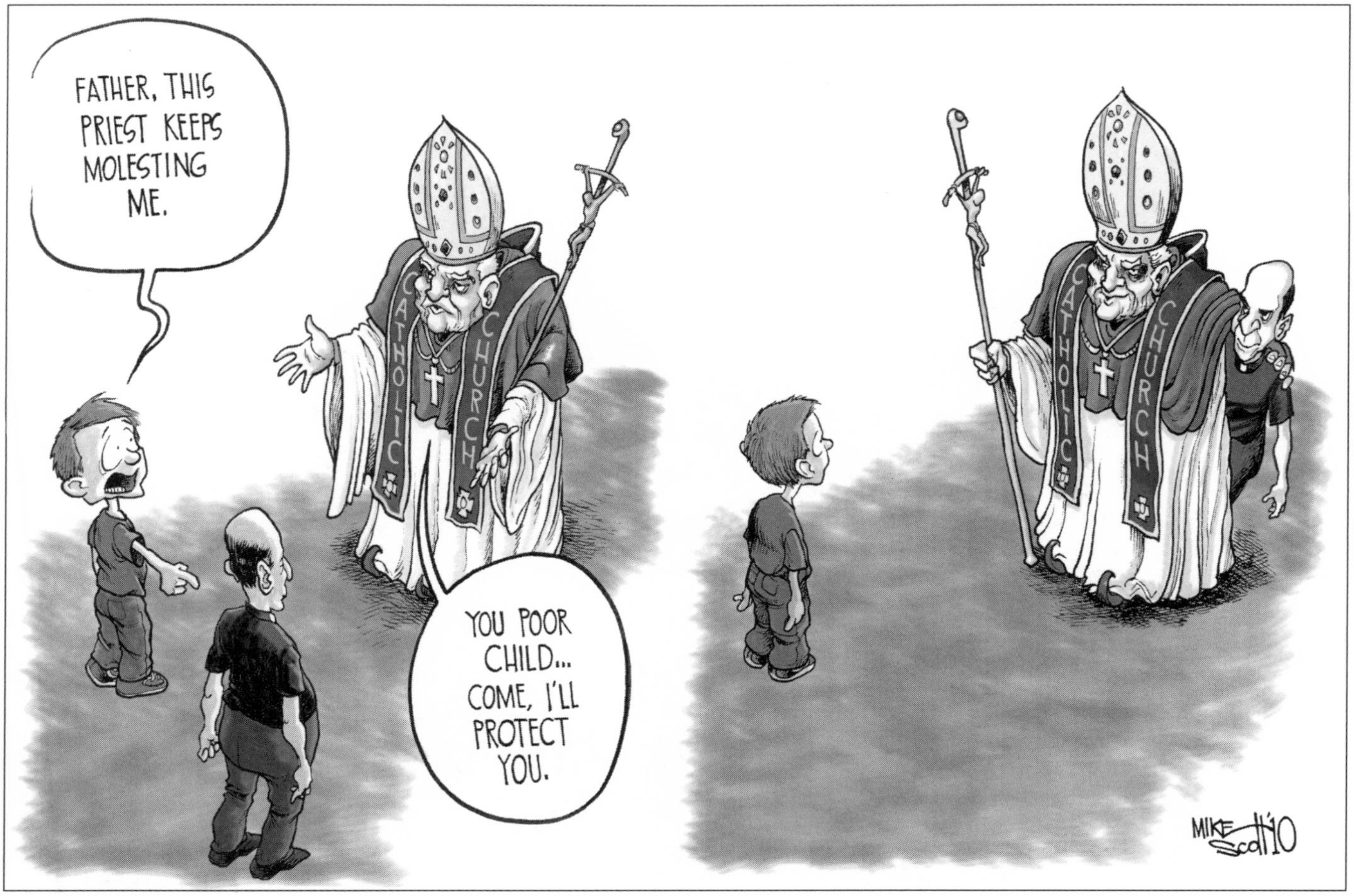
FATHER, THIS PRIEST KEEPS MOLESTING ME.
CATHOLIC CHURCH
YOU POOR CHILD... COME, I'LL PROTECT YOU.
CATHOLIC CHURCH
MIKE Scott '10

STEVE KELLEY
Courtesy Times-Picayune (La.)

STEVE BREEN
Courtesy San Diego Union-Tribune

Past Award Winners

PULITZER PRIZE

1922—Rollin Kirby, New York World
1923—No award given
1924—J.N. Darling, New York Herald-Tribune
1925—Rollin Kirby, New York World
1926—D.R. Fitzpatrick, St. Louis Post-Dispatch
1927—Nelson Harding, Brooklyn Eagle
1928—Nelson Harding, Brooklyn Eagle
1929—Rollin Kirby, New York World
1930—Charles Macauley, Brooklyn Eagle
1931—Edmund Duffy, Baltimore Sun
1932—John T. McCutcheon, Chicago Tribune
1933—H.M. Talburt, Washington Daily News
1934—Edmund Duffy, Baltimore Sun
1935—Ross A. Lewis, Milwaukee Journal
1936—No award given
1937—C.D. Batchelor, New York Daily News
1938—Vaughn Shoemaker, Chicago Daily News
1939—Charles G. Werner, Daily Oklahoman
1940—Edmund Duffy, Baltimore Sun
1941—Jacob Burck, Chicago Times
1942—Herbert L. Block, NEA
1943—Jay N. Darling, New York Herald-Tribune
1944—Clifford K. Berryman, Washington Star
1945—Bill Mauldin, United Features Syndicate
1946—Bruce Russell, Los Angeles Times
1947—Vaughn Shoemaker, Chicago Daily News
1948—Reuben L. ("Rube") Goldberg, New York Sun
1949—Lute Pease, Newark Evening News
1950—James T. Berryman, Washington Star
1951—Reginald W. Manning, Arizona Republic
1952—Fred L. Packer, New York Mirror
1953—Edward D. Kuekes, Cleveland Plain Dealer
1954—Herbert L. Block, Washington Post
1955—Daniel R. Fitzpatrick, St. Louis Post-Dispatch
1956—Robert York, Louisville Times
1957—Tom Little, Nashville Tennessean
1958—Bruce M. Shanks, Buffalo Evening News
1959—Bill Mauldin, St. Louis Post-Dispatch
1960—No award given
1961—Carey Orr, Chicago Tribune
1962—Edmund S. Valtman, Hartford Times
1963—Frank Miller, Des Moines Register
1964—Paul Conrad, Denver Post
1965—No award given
1966—Don Wright, Miami News
1967—Patrick B. Oliphant, Denver Post

1968—Eugene Gray Payne, Charlotte Observer
1969—John Fischetti, Chicago Daily News
1970—Thomas F. Darcy, Newsday
1971—Paul Conrad, Los Angeles Times
1972—Jeffrey K. MacNelly, Richmond News Leader
1973—No award given
1974—Paul Szep, Boston Globe
1975—Garry Trudeau, Universal Press Syndicate
1976—Tony Auth, Philadelphia Enquirer
1977—Paul Szep, Boston Globe
1978—Jeff MacNelly, Richmond News Leader
1979—Herbert Block, Washington Post
1980—Don Wright, Miami News
1981—Mike Peters, Dayton Daily News
1982—Ben Sargent, Austin American-Statesman
1983—Dick Locher, Chicago Tribune
1984—Paul Conrad, Los Angeles Times
1985—Jeff MacNelly, Chicago Tribune
1986—Jules Feiffer, Universal Press Syndicate
1987—Berke Breathed, Washington Post Writers Group
1988—Doug Marlette, Atlanta Constitution
1989—Jack Higgins, Chicago Sun-Times
1990—Tom Toles, Buffalo News
1991—Jim Borgman, Cincinnati Enquirer
1992—Signe Wilkinson, Philadelphia Daily News
1993—Steve Benson, Arizona Republic
1994—Michael Ramirez, Memphis Commercial Appeal
1995—Mike Luckovich, Atlanta Constitution
1996—Jim Morin, Miami Herald
1997—Walt Handelsman, New Orleans Times-Picayune
1998—Steve Breen, Asbury Park Press
1999—David Horsey, Seattle Post-Intelligencer
2000—Joel Pett, Lexington Herald-Leader
2001—Ann Telnaes, Tribune Media Services
2002—Clay Bennett, Christian Science Monitor
2003—David Horsey, Seattle Post-Intelligencer
2004—Matt Davies, The Journal News
2005—Nick Anderson, Louisville Courier-Journal
2006—Mike Luckovich, Atlanta Journal-Constitution
2007—Walt Handelsman, Newsday
2008—Michael Ramirez, Investors Business Daily
2009—Steve Breen, San Diego Tribune
2010—Mark Fiore, SFGate.com

SIGMA DELTA CHI AWARD

1942—Jacob Burck, Chicago Times
1943—Charles Werner, Chicago Sun
1944—Henry Barrow, Associated Press
1945—Reuben L. Goldberg, New York Sun
1946—Dorman H. Smith, NEA
1947—Bruce Russell, Los Angeles Times
1948—Herbert Block, Washington Post
1949—Herbert Block, Washington Post
1950—Bruce Russell, Los Angeles Times
1951—Herbert Block, Washington Post and
      Bruce Russell, Los Angeles Times
1952—Cecil Jensen, Chicago Daily News
1953—John Fischetti, NEA
1954—Calvin Alley, Memphis Commercial Appeal
1955—John Fischetti, NEA
1956—Herbert Block, Washington Post
1957—Scott Long, Minneapolis Tribune
1958—Clifford H. Baldowski, Atlanta Constitution
1959—Charles G. Brooks, Birmingham News
1960—Dan Dowling, New York Herald-Tribune
1961—Frank Interlandi, Des Moines Register
1962—Paul Conrad, Denver Post
1963—William Mauldin, Chicago Sun-Times
1964—Charles Bissell, Nashville Tennessean
1965—Roy Justus, Minneapolis Star
1966—Patrick Oliphant, Denver Post
1967—Eugene Payne, Charlotte Observer
1968—Paul Conrad, Los Angeles Times
1969—William Mauldin, Chicago Sun-Times
1970—Paul Conrad, Los Angeles Times
1971—Hugh Haynie, Louisville Courier-Journal
1972—William Mauldin, Chicago Sun-Times
1973—Paul Szep, Boston Globe
1974—Mike Peters, Dayton Daily News
1975—Tony Auth, Philadelphia Enquirer

1976—Paul Szep, Boston Globe
1977—Don Wright, Miami News
1978—Jim Borgman, Cincinnati Enquirer
1979—John P. Trever, Albuquerque Journal
1980—Paul Conrad, Los Angeles Times
1981—Paul Conrad, Los Angeles Times
1982—Dick Locher, Chicago Tribune
1983—Rob Lawlor, Philadelphia Daily News
1984—Mike Lane, Baltimore Evening Sun
1985—Doug Marlette, Charlotte Observer
1986—Mike Keefe, Denver Post
1987—Paul Conrad, Los Angeles Times
1988—Jack Higgins, Chicago Sun-Times
1989—Don Wright, Palm Beach Post
1990—Jeff MacNelly, Chicago Tribune
1991—Walt Handelsman, New Orleans Times-
      Picayune
1992—Robert Ariail, Columbia State
1993—Herbert Block, Washington Post
1994—Jim Borgman, Cincinnati Enquirer
1995—Michael Ramirez, Memphis Commercial
      Appeal
1996—Paul Conrad, Los Angeles Times
1997—Michael Ramirez, Los Angeles Times
1998—Jack Higgins, Chicago Sun-Times
1999—Mike Thompson, Detroit Free Press
2000—Nick Anderson, Louisville Courier-Journal
2001—Clay Bennett, Christian Science Monitor
2002—Mike Thompson, Detroit Free Press
2003—Steve Sack, Minneapolis Star-Tribune
2004—John Sherffius, jsherffius@aol.com
2005—Mike Luckovich, Atlanta Journal-Constitution
2006—Mike Lester, Rome News-Tribune
2007—Michael Ramirez, Investors Business Daily
2008—Chris Britt, State Journal-Register
2009—Jack Ohman, The Oregonian

Index of Cartoonists

Complete Your CARTOON COLLECTION

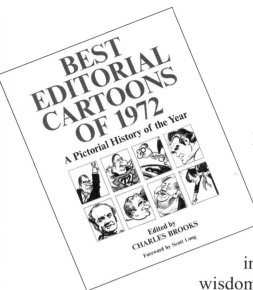

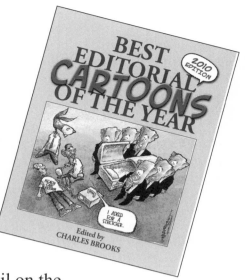

Previous editions of this timeless classic are available for those wishing to update their collection of the most provocative moments of the past four decades. Most important, in the end, the wit and wisdom of the editorial cartoonists prevail on the pages of these op-ed editorials, where one can find memories and much, much more in the work of the nation's finest cartoonists.

Select from the following supply of past editions

____1972 Edition	$20.00 pb (F)	____1987 Edition	$20.00 pb	____2001 Edition	$20.00 pb
____1974 Edition	$20.00 pb (F)	____1988 Edition	$20.00 pb	____2002 Edition	$14.95 pb
____1975 Edition	$20.00 pb (F)	____1989 Edition	$20.00 pb (F)	____2003 Edition	$14.95 pb
____1976 Edition	$20.00 pb (F)	____1990 Edition	$20.00 pb	____2004 Edition	$14.95 pb
____1977 Edition	$20.00 pb (F)	____1991 Edition	$20.00 pb	____2005 Edition	$14.95 pb
____1978 Edition	$20.00 pb (F)	____1992 Edition	$20.00 pb	____2006 Edition	$14.95 pb
____1979 Edition	$20.00 pb (F)	____1993 Edition	$20.00 pb	____2007 Edition	$14.95 pb
____1980 Edition	$20.00 pb (F)	____1994 Edition	$20.00 pb	____2008 Edition	$14.95 pb
____1981 Edition	$20.00 pb (F)	____1995 Edition	$20.00 pb	____2009 Edition	$14.95 pb
____1982 Edition	$20.00 pb (F)	____1996 Edition	$20.00 pb	____2010 Edition	$14.95 pb
____1983 Edition	$20.00 pb (F)	____1997 Edition	$20.00 pb		
____1984 Edition	$20.00 pb (F)	____1998 Edition	$20.00 pb		
____1985 Edition	$20.00 pb (F)	____1999 Edition	$20.00 pb	____Add me to the list of standing	
____1986 Edition	$20.00 pb (F)	____2000 Edition	$20.00 pb	orders	

Please include $2.95 for 4th Class Postage and handling or $6.85 for UPS Ground Shipment plus $.75 for each additional copy ordered.

Total enclosed: _____

NAME _____

ADDRESS _____

CITY_____ STATE _____ ZIP_____

Make checks payable to:

PELICAN PUBLISHING COMPANY
1000 Burmaster St, Dept. 6BEC
Gretna, Louisiana 70053-2246

CREDIT CARD ORDERS CALL 1-800-843-1724 or or go to pelicanpub.com
Jefferson Parish residents add 8¾% tax. All other Louisiana residents add 4% tax.
Please visit our Web site at www.pelicanpub.com or e-mail us at sales@pelicanpub.com